THE *POWER* OF THE *PITCH*

THE POWER OF THE PITCH

OF THE PITCH

TRANSFORM YOURSELF INTO A PERSUASIVE PRESENTER AND WIN MORE BUSINESS

Gary Hankins

Dearborn™
Trade Publishing
A **Kaplan Professional** Company

Vice President and Publisher: Cynthia A. Zigmund
Acquisitions Editor: Michael Cunningham
Senior Project Editor: Trey Thoelcke
Interior Design: Lucy Jenkins
Cover Design: Scott Rattray, Rattray Design
Typesetting: the dotted i

Published by Dearborn Trade Publishing
A Kaplan Professional Company

Printed in the United States of America

05 06 07   10 9 8 7 6 5 4 3 2 1

Library of Congress Cataloging-in-Publication Data

Hankins, Gary, 1945-
    The power of the pitch : transform yourself into a more persuasive
presenter and win more business / Gary Hankins.
        p.   cm.
    Includes bibliographical references and index.
    ISBN 0-7931-9439-3
    1. Business presentations.   I. Title.
HF5718.22.H356 2005
658.8′2—dc22

                                                                2004015642

Dearborn Trade books are available at special quantity discounts to use for sales promotions, employee premiums, or educational purposes. Please call our Special Sales Department to order or for more information at 800-621-9621 ext. 4444, e-mail trade@dearborn.com, or write to Dearborn Trade Publishing, 30 South Wacker Drive, Suite 2500, Chicago, IL 60606-7481.

Praise for *The Power of the Pitch*

"*The Power of the Pitch* incorporates the tremendously valuable strategies, tools and techniques Gary Hankins has been teaching our professionals over the past decade into one neat package. I recommend his book to everyone who makes a living by persuading others to see their point of view."
John C. Cushman III, Chairman of the Board, Cushman & Wakefield

"There *is* power in the pitch, and the Pygmalion concepts help unleash it! Having been through the coaching experience with Gary Hankins, I can attest to the effectiveness of the concepts outlined in this book. Incorporating just a few of them will enable readers to become more confident—and more effective—in any business environment."
Burv Pugh, Senior Vice President, Retail Distribution, MassMutual Financial Group

"Anyone who thinks public speaking is more frightening than jumping from a plane will go out and buy a flight suit after reading Gary's book. This book is fresh, clear, practical, insightful, and humorous. It is a must for anyone who aspires to leadership, through public speaking."
Robert J. Dowling, Publisher and Editor in Chief, *Hollywood Reporter*

"Gary Hankins is a marvelous teacher of powerful speaking fundamentals that can be very beneficial to speakers and presenters of all levels. His book and program are a must for all those seeking to improve their speaking skills."
Terry Donahue, General Manager, San Francisco 49ers

"We have used Garry Hankins' principals and methodology right across Asia Pacific for a number of years, and they work. The lifeblood of any service organization is satisfying and retaining your current clients and attracting and winning new ones. *The Power of the Pitch* is equally relevant for both groups. Whether its our client relationship managers or business developers in India, China, Singapore, Australia, or any of our 25 offices, the skills Garry has taught us and detailed in the book are a big part of what makes our people market leaders."

Peter Barge, CEO, Asia Pacific, Jones Lang LaSalle

"I am in the business of pitching shows to TV networks. I needed to be a better closer. *The Power of the Pitch* helped me fine tune and focus my presentations. The results speak for themselves."

Eugene Young, Senior Vice President, Programming and Development, Endemol USA, Producers of *Fear Factor*, *Big Brother*, and *Extreme Makeover*, *Home Edition*

"Gary's book condenses into writing what he has been coaching our partners to do for years. His insights and approach are clear and to the point, and allow our partners to be more effective in serving our clients and communicating with our people. Gary's insights are an important element of our professionals' development and success."

Tony Buzzelli, Office Managing Partner, Deloitte & Touche

Gary's book serves as a detailed guide to making presentations while providing important "life lessons" along the way. It is immensely readable and informative. I highly recommend it to anyone who wants to improve their public performances to a world class level."

Larry Hirsch, Former Chairman and CEO, Centex Corporation

"*The Power of the Pitch* allows us to add the way we present to our list of competitive advantages. *The Power of the Pitch* is an excellent vehicle to teach new sales people critical presentation skills and allow experienced salespeople to fine tune their skills."

William L. MacDonald, Chairman, President, and CEO, Retirement Capital Group, Inc.

"Gary Hankins has distilled the essence of a successful pitch. *The Power of the Pitch* should be required reading for anyone who intends to successfully communicate. I will keep this book in my office as an integral part of my reference library."

Allan Anderson, Resident Director and Business Litigation Partner, Ropers, Majeski, Kohn & Bentley

"Having the benefit of Gary Hankins's wisdom early in my career was fortuitous. Gary's lessons have become an integral part of training in the businesses and organizations in which I hold leadership positions. His message is useful to every person in his or her professional and personal life. Even my sixteen-year-old daughter preparing for college entrance interviews has benefited from Gary's teachings. Thankfully Gary has put his message in writing. Those who read *The Power of the Pitch* will increase their opportunities for success."

Brian R. Kroh, CCM, General Manager, John's Island Club, and Director, National Club Association

Dedicated to **Gabi Hankins,** my beautiful daughter, and **Betty Hankins,** my loving mother, who have taught me so much about love and life

Presentations Magazine estimates that businessmen and women give over one million presentations in the United States every business day. When you factor in the cities worldwide, the number of presentations could easily be in the tens of millions. Most of those presentations are intended to be persuasive and, unfortunately, most fail miserably—not due to lack of knowledge or experience but because presenters don't place a premium on the power of the persuasive presentation, the pitch. Typically, sales professionals spend most of their time prospecting and convincing decision makers to see them. Senior executives devote most of their time dealing with the day-to-day challenges of business. Appointments made and meetings scheduled, they turn their attention to preparing written proposals or PowerPoint slides. They save the most important part, preparing a powerful pitch that will cause the audience to do what they want, for a hurried discussion on the way to the meeting.

Complicating matters is the entry of Web conferencing. Because this efficient medium eliminates the expense and time of travel, Web conferencing has the potential of dwarfing in-person meetings. *Forbes* magazine named WebEx, the largest provider of Web communications services, the number one fastest growing company in 2003. Gartner Research opined that Microsoft's acquisition of Web conferencing provider Placeware will dramatically change the industry. Frost and Little estimates that Web conferencing will grow from $266 million in 2001 to $2 billion by 2010.

The combination of in-person and Web conferencing meetings means that within the next two years you will be making two or three times as many pitches as you are today. Without question, your ability to make a persuasive presentation will become much more important tomorrow than it is today. The unique formula in this book guarantees the success of your pitches, now and in the future.

The same strategies and skills that I used to coach thousands of sales professionals, executives, and sports personalities are the ones you will learn in this book. Unlike most communication books, *The Power of the Pitch* provides you with a comprehensive, time tested formula that you must follow from the moment you make an appointment to the moment the prospect, client, or team member says, "Yes." I suggest you read this book sequentially— from the first chapter to the last. You'll find that most chapters build on the previous one. After you've read all the chapters, use this book as a handy reference for specific areas of your pitch that you feel you could improve.

I developed the concepts in this book over a 30-year period that started when, as a second lieutenant, I taught presentation skills to the U.S. Army. After the military, I employed the strategies in this book to build a successful securities business. During my 15-year career as a stockbroker serving wealthy investors, I gave thousands of sales presentations, hundreds of speeches, and hosted my own radio and television shows. All the while, I refined and enhanced the tools, strategies, and concepts you are about to learn.

Recognizing that my passion was speaking to audiences of any size and that my calling in life was to help people become the most powerful communicators they could be, I founded Pygmalion Inc. in 1988. Since then, I have coached and conducted workshops for many Fortune 500 companies, associations, and collegiate and professional sports teams. My programs based on the concepts in this book consistently receive the highest ratings from such groups as the Young Presidents Organization, the National Football League, Deloitte Touche Tohmatsu, Jones Lang LaSalle, and Cushman & Wakefield.

During my professional coaching and speaking career, I have continued to refine the concepts in this book. Now, for the first time ever, you will have a comprehensive, time-tested method for creating and delivering successful pitches. Everything you need to know to persuade people to do what you want them to do is contained in this book. Follow the principles in this book and you will win more business. Stay tuned; you are about to learn how to make persuasive presentations that will make you and your organization more money than you dreamed possible.

- Betsy Green, to whom I shall be eternally grateful
- Peter Barge, Jones Lang LaSalle
- Mary Lin Dedeaux, Image Consultant
- My friends who gladly served as models:
  - Michael Angel
  - Dreaux McNairy
  - Bruce Murdoch
  - Jay Richardson
  - Ted Simpson
  - Charlie Smith
  - Miyuki Smith

1

THE SECRETS OF
WINNING PEOPLE OVER

Dateline: September 26, 1960, 6:00 PM
U.S. Vice President Richard M. Nixon arrives at a Chicago television station. He's tired, ill, and running a fever after two weeks of heavy campaigning.

Moments earlier, in his hotel room, Nixon's advisors pleaded with him to cancel the evening's activities. Sensing that Nixon, the fighter, would continue, his advisors told him that the background in the studio was a dark gray and that he should wear a light gray suit for sharp contrast. As Nixon and his advisors enter the studio, they are shocked to see that the backdrop is light gray.

The producers are surprised to see that Nixon hasn't shaved since early that morning. To make matters worse, he refuses to go to makeup. Finally, moments before he goes on the air, he agrees to let the producers apply a thin coating of Lazy Shave over the dark stubble of his beard.

At 7:00 PM Howard K. Smith welcomes 70 million people, the largest television audience since the World Series the year before, to watch the first televised presidential debate featuring the ailing

Nixon and a relatively unknown senator by the name of John F. Kennedy. The first question goes to Nixon. He looks tired, distraught, almost frightened. His light gray suit blends in with the backdrop.

The second question goes to Kennedy. He's cool, calm, and crisp in a navy blue suit. On this evening, absent are many of the distractions that Kennedy typically had. Under pressure, he would frequently tug at his tie and stroke his face. If he were sitting down, he would slap his knee in an awkward manner. Tonight, none of these distractions are present.

The debate continues. Then something very interesting happens. Halfway through the program, under the hot lights of the television studio, Nixon's fever breaks. Beads of perspiration form on his forehead and trickle down the side of his face making tracks in the Lazy Shave. Those watching the program were amazed to see Nixon falling apart under the strain of the debate with Kennedy. It was a long, arduous evening for Nixon.

Those who listened to the radio thought it was even and that both candidates presented themselves equally well. Those who watched television came away with a far different point of view. The next morning newspapers reported that the gallop poll picked the winner:

- Kennedy 43 percent
- Nixon 23 percent

Not only did Nixon lose the first debate, he didn't do well on the following two debates and, of course, he lost the election. So, how could Nixon have lost? Throughout his life, Nixon was tremendous on his feet: on the college debate team, throughout law school, in Congress, first in the House of Representatives and then in the Senate, and then as one of the most visible vice presidents in the United States. Kennedy, on the other hand, was relatively unknown and thought to be a bit of a playboy. So why did Nixon lose? He lost for one basic reason . . . we didn't like him.

THE POWER OF LIKEABILITY

The most important rule in making a successful pitch is that people must like you. Specifically, they must like three qualities that define you. If they don't, they won't listen to you, vote for you, be persuaded by you, or buy your products or services. The three elements, in order of importance, are:

1. How you look
2. How you sound
3. What you say

A study by Professor Albert Mehrabian of Stanford and UCLA concludes that your appearance accounts for 55 percent of your total likeability; your voice, 38 percent; and your message, 7 percent. Although Dr. Mehrabian based his research on interpersonal communication, he informed me that he was confident the results would be the same for presentations an individual would make to any number of people.

Contrary to Dr. Mehrabian's study, Nixon thought that his message was the most important part of the debate. Apparently, the people who listened to the radio thought so, too. But those who watched television proved Mehrabian's point: people will decide whether they like you or not primarily based on how you look and sound.

Richard Nixon made thousands of personal appearances during his political life but none as important as the debate on the evening of September 26, 1960. In its purest form, the debate was a pitch for the most powerful elected post in the free world.

His weak presentation derailed his progress and nearly ended his career as a public servant. It was this single event that brought William Shakespeare's assertion that "all the world's a stage" into the 21st century. Nixon now realized that every person in the world would scrutinize his pitches. If he wanted to become president of the United States of America, he had to pay close attention to not only what he said, but also to how he looked and sounded.

Once, while I was speaking at a State Bar of California annual conference in San Francisco, a lawyer at the back of the room raised his hand just as I had quoted the percentages from the Mehrabian study.

"Mr. Hankins," announced the man in a bellowing voice as he stood to address me, "let me see if I understand you correctly. Are you telling us that a jury will make a decision primarily based on how we look and sound? Is that what you're telling us?"

I said, "That's exactly right."

"Well," he continued, "if that's the case, why don't we just stand up, look good, smile, say, 'Good morning,' and sit down? Why risk it? Why say anything?" As he took his seat, the room exploded in laughter.

Although there is some truth in what the lawyer said, it's only partially accurate. Yes, how you look and sound are the most important elements of likeability. But once people like these two parts, they will focus on what you say. Now the message becomes tremendously important. We must be sure that we get these parts about how we look and how we sound right so that people will focus on the message itself.

THE ROCK STAR ATTITUDE

Garth Brooks was a struggling country singer desperate to sign a record contract when he arrived in Nashville in 1987. He had played the honky-tonk bars of Oklahoma and, at the age of 25, this was his second attempt to make it in the big city. Determined to do whatever it took to gain visibility, he played in clubs seven nights a week.

Through a contact, Brooks arranged a meeting with a well-known, influential record producer. This could be his big break. After the meeting, Brooks was fuming when he reported the encounter to a songwriter friend. The producer had told Garth that, although he was talented, he didn't want to work with him because there wasn't "enough love" in what Brooks did. The friend told Garth that there was some truth in what the producer said. "When you're on that stage," he advised Garth, "you want the audience to like you. But, you have to like them first. You have to

Garth Brooks

find something to like in each one of them. If you do, they can't help but to like you back." Garth took this advice to heart. He began to give "love" to his audiences in his live performances. Within two years, he signed a record contract with Capital Records. Today, Garth Brooks is the biggest selling solo recording artist in the United States. He has even sold more records than the Beatles. His fiercely loyal fans have shattered the concert attendance records of Elvis Presley, the Rolling Stones, the Grateful Dead, and Elton John.

Another performer who embodies the Rock Star Attitude is Bruce Springsteen. This gravel voiced, middle-aged man continues to break music record sales and sell out concerts in a matter of hours. Why do fans pay thousands of dollars for scalpers' front row tickets? It's

Bruce Springsteen

simple: Bruce Springsteen gives his audience two and one-half hours of high-energy rock'n'roll. As if that weren't enough, he and his E Street Band always come back to perform an encore. His interaction with the fans and commitment to play until he drops has earned him rock star icon status. He has been known to perform for three and one-half hours, but that's usually in his home state of New Jersey or in Madison Square Garden, where many consider him a local hero, if not a national treasure. Like Garth Brooks, Bruce Springsteen understands the importance of giving his audiences love. The same can be said for Erykah Badu, Beyonce Knowles, and Outkast, all of whom have huge followings.

For you to win more business, you, too, must have this same attitude. You must show your customers and prospects that you like them so they will reciprocate and like you. If you don't give them some love, they will not like you. If they don't like you, they won't buy. Period.

There are numerous studies to add credence to the principle of the Rock Star Attitude. The State Bar of Missouri, a number of years ago, conducted one of the most poignant studies in which it sent out a survey to all the attorneys and their clients in the state. There was one question that was particularity relevant: What do clients want in an attorney-client relationship? Or simply, what do clients want from their lawyers? In order of importance, the attorney respondents said:

1. Results
2. Honesty

3. Efficiency
4. Personality
5. Education

Interestingly, clients answered the question quite differently:

1. *Friendliness*. Clients wanted attorneys to be friendly to them. "It's OK not to be friendly to the opposing parties," they said, "but you'd better be friendly to us."
2. *Promptness*. This is usually the number one complaint registered with state bars: attorneys don't return phone calls promptly.
3. *Courtesy*. Clients want lawyers who say "please" and "thank you."
4. *Empathy*. Clients want attorneys who care about them. It's not just about billable hours.
5. *Informative*. Clients want to be kept up to date.

Why do you think clients' responses were so different from those of the attorneys? Why didn't clients list *results* at all? The answer is that producing results is assumed. Once you've gone through the due diligence and selected a lawyer, you expect that lawyer to perform.

Here's the follow up question I have for you: Do you think the responses clients gave for what they were looking for in lawyers is similar to what your clients expect from you? Absolutely! However, as important as expressing the Rock Star Attitude is, many people never get it. You see it every day: the grocery store cashier who barely acknowledges your presence, the rude airline attendant who is too busy to get you a blanket, the surly waiter who acts like he's doing you a favor when you ask for a glass of water. After one of these or any of the dozens of experiences that you encounter during an average year, you may say to yourself, "I'm never coming back here again." Meanwhile, the companies that employ these individuals each spent thousands of dollars, euros, or yen just to get you in the door, and with one attitude, it's all gone right down the drain.

According to a study conducted by McDonalds Corporation, the impact is far greater than the advertising costs companies spend to attract customers. For every pleasant experience a customer has, he or she will tell just two people. But, for every bad experience, a customer will tell ten people. You can't afford to have that kind of a negative public relations program going for you.

THE 30-SECOND CLOCK

How long does it take for you to decide if you like somebody? If you're like the average person, it can be very quick. An office equipment salesman enters your office and takes a seat. Before he begins his presentation, you've decided. It can be a matter of seconds, perhaps up to 30 seconds.

As a presenter, you will be held to the same 30-second clock. Suppose you enter a prospect's conference room to pitch your company's services to six executives. As you begin your presentation, the executives mentally click their stop watches to begin the count. Ten seconds elapse. The woman seated to your left is thinking, "I don't think she is interested in me." Fifteen seconds elapse. The man to your right is thinking, "She looks nervous. I'm beginning to feel uncomfortable." Twenty seconds. The man seated directly in front of you is thinking, "She has a big ego. I'm not going to enjoy working with her." Tick, tick, tick. The second hand touches 30 and silent buzzers go off with the kind of intensity that alerts nuclear power plant engineers of potential accidents. Time is up and guess what? You lose. It's over.

A man on the street confirmed the importance of the 30-second clock. One morning I was walking along the sidewalk in downtown Los Angeles and noticed that an attorney I had seen around town was just a few steps behind me. I slowed down and introduced myself.

"I'm Mike Axle," the man offered in return.

"What do you do, Mike?" I asked.

"I'm a senior partner at a major law firm," Mike responded. "How about you?"

"I help people become powerful communicators," I said.

"That is so important!" Mike said emphatically. "Last week we won one of the biggest cases in our firm's history. Afterward we interviewed several jurors to see what they liked about the way we presented our argument and how we might have improved it. One woman said to me, 'I knew you were going to win when I saw your partner enter the courtroom.' Within a matter of seconds she decided she liked my partner, could trust him, and was willing to cast her ballot in our client's favor. That's pretty amazing."

THE PITCH

A pitch is defined as *any time you speak with the intent to persuade.* Pitches could be delivered in person, over the telephone, to one person or to thousands. Here are some examples of pitches:

- Sales presentations
- Fund raising presentations
- Breakfast, lunch, or dinner meetings with prospects and clients
- Speeches at a conference
- Television interviews
- Motivational presentations to your team
- Discussions with your friends and family

- Video and Web conferences with prospects and clients
- Interviews for a new job

When you think about it, you make pitches all the time—perhaps dozens throughout the day. Many are casual, informal pitches to family, friends, and business associates. Some are more structured pitches to prospects and customers for new or additional business. For all of these venues and more, you are on your way to becoming a persuasive presenter capable of winning more business.

2

BE THE BRAND

ME? A BRAND?

You may be asking yourself, "Can I create my own personal brand? And if so, how?" Before we tackle these questions, let's establish a definition of brand.

Brand: The perception people have of the experience of having a relationship with you

Pay particular attention to the word *perception*. To help you grasp the significance of perception in creating your brand, I'll begin with a few questions. Ready?

When you look at the logos at left, what words come to mind?

NORDSTROM

Salvatore Ferragamo

With Nordstrom, you may think of service. For Ferragamo, it may be quality and style. These companies have one thing in common: they have established powerful brands.

How about individuals? Do they have brands, too? Absolutely! Think about the words you would use to describe each of the following.

Marines, Abraham Lincoln, Mother Teresa, and Albert Einstein

For the Marines, you might say discipline; for Albert Einstein, intelligence; for Abraham Lincoln, honesty; and for Mother Teresa, humanitarianism.

Here's the more difficult question: When clients describe you, what would they say? Just like successful corporations and well-known individuals, it's vital that you clearly define and promote a powerful brand. If you do not have an identifiable brand, you will be perceived as a commodity in the marketplace that trades on the basis of price.

If you are a representative of a company, your brand must be in sync with your company's brand. Prospects and clients typically will request that your company, not you personally, make a pitch to them. Perhaps your firm will ask you to be one of the members of a presentation team. When you make your pitch, you and your team members must look like you're on the same team. If you appear to be on different teams, the audience will have a mixed perception of your corporate brand. Imagine one of your teammates in a San Francisco 49ers uniform, another in a Green Bay Packers uniform, a third teammate in an Atlanta Falcons uniform, and you in a Tampa Bay Buccaneers uniform. If your team is perceived as divergent and with no clear identity, you will lose the business.

The idea of creating a perception that defines your brand isn't new. One of the most famous stories about the importance of perception dates back to Greek mythology and the famous story of the Greek god, Pygmalion. Pygmalion created an ivory statue of a woman and made her so beautiful that he fell in love with her. He courted her with flowers, precious gifts, and undying affection. During the Festival of Aphrodite, Pygmalion promised that if Aphrodite would bring the statute to life, he would marry her and shower her with love and affection forever. Aphrodite granted Pygmalion his wish, and Pygmalion carried out his pledge of marriage and everlasting love.

In 1913, George Bernard Shaw published a play, *Pygmalion*, which made wildly successful transitions into film and theater under the name *My Fair Lady*. In *Pygmalion*, as in *My Fair Lady*, the confident phoeneticist Professor Henry Higgins wagers that under his tutelage, cockney flower girl Eliza Doolittle can pass for a duchess at the Embassy Ball. So successful is Higgins that his self-proclaimed best student, Count Esteed Nepommuck, proclaims to the Queen and her court, "She is a princess."

Was she really a princess? No. She was a woman who sold flowers on the streets of London. But she was *perceived* to be a princess.

Perception is important because perception is reality. The way people perceive you is the way they believe you are—and they aren't going to follow you home and spend weeks with you to confirm their beliefs. They're going to observe you during a short period of time—perhaps an hour or less—and come to a conclusion about you. That perception is their reality. You need to be sure that the perception you create for people is the one you want.

Unfortunately, sometimes we create the wrong perception. One of my favorite television commercials illustrates this point perfectly. The scene opens with an attractive blonde in a red bathing suit standing on the beach scanning the water. The camera pans to the ocean where a man is bobbing in the water, yelling for help. A caption appears under the scene, "Pretending to drown." The camera pans back to the woman in the bathing suit. The caption reads, "Not a lifeguard." The camera then pans to the lifeguard tower where an overweight man with scraggly hair comes racing down from the lifeguard tower, life buoy in tow. The voiceover proclaims, "There's our lifeguard. And he loves giving CPR."

History is filled with people who have created the wrong perceptions. As with Eliza Doolittle, many have undergone major transformations in an effort to change the perceptions people had of them. One of the most profound modern examples of transformation is that of former First Lady Hillary Rodham Clinton. During Bill Clinton's first term as the governor of Arkansas, Mrs. Clinton wore paisley dresses, large horn-rimmed glasses, and her hair in an unattractive, mousy manner. After her husband lost the governorship in his bid for a second term, she upgraded her wardrobe to smart, tailored suits, lost the glasses, and coiffed and lightened her hair. Clearly she realized that the way voters perceived her was important, too. Bill Clinton was reelected governor on his next attempt, thanks in part to Mrs. Clinton's new brand image.

THE BASIS OF PERCEPTION

There are numerous factors upon which people will base their perceptions of you. Here are just a few:

- Attention to detail
- Health
- Social status
- Self-confidence
- Taste
- Financial status
- Family background
- Education
- Trustworthiness
- Level of success

With computer-like speed, your clients' and prospects' minds will race through a list of 50 plus factors as they formulate their perceptions of you. In 30 seconds or less, they will have the answer. Will it be the one you want them to have?

ONSTAGE VERSUS OFFSTAGE

In theater, when actors perform on a stage before an audience, they are *onstage*. When they disappear behind the curtain, they are *offstage* or backstage. When actors are onstage, the audience is keenly aware of their presence, even when they are not speaking. As a result, actors have been directed on how they must stand and move and what facial expressions they must have. Miscues and straying from the script could prove disastrous.

This same concept of onstage versus offstage applies to business, too. There is no corporation more aware of this notion than Disney. The people who work at Disneyland and Disney World are not employees, they're actors. When a Disney actor is dressing, she is *offstage.* When she leaves her dressing room to begin her work, she passes through the *stage door.* Once through, she is *onstage.* On a recent visit to Disneyland, I noticed one of the actors sweeping the sidewalk. This would normally be no major moment, except that when I looked closer, I saw what he was sweeping. Nothing. The place was so clean that he didn't have any trash to sweep, so he was pretending to sweep. His actions further enhanced the perception of cleanliness, for which Disney theme parks are known.

It doesn't matter if you're demonstrating the latest features of a new model automobile or discussing your marketing plan for a new consumer product, prospects will observe your every move and word. The characteristics about you that you don't think about, such as the expressions on your face, the tone of your voice and the words you use to describe your uniqueness, are all under a giant mobile magnifying glass.

The stages for your pitches may include:

- Your office
- A client or prospect's lobby
- A client or prospect's office
- A restaurant
- A conference room
- A television studio
- An auditorium

- Your car
- An airplane
- The street
- A sporting event
- A dinner party
- The telephone
- Your home
- A client's home
- A parking lot

Yes, even your client's parking lot is a stage. Betsy Green found that out at age 24 in her job selling syndicated television shows. One morning she arrived at the building occupied by a prospective client. As she got out of her car, she checked her makeup, combed her hair, and blew her nose. When she met the new prospect, he was laughing. Instead of saying a word, he peered into a small mirror as if to check makeup, combed his hair, and blew his nose. "I watched the whole thing," he confided as Betsy turned a bright shade of red.

Wherever you are, people are gaining a perception of you. If you've just had lunch and blackberry seeds are lodged between your teeth, your afternoon appointment will perceive you as careless and inattentive to details. If you speak too slowly and deliberately, the television audience may perceive that you're speaking down to them, as was the case with former U.S. Vice President Al Gore. If you use the wrong words, people may perceive you as being unintelligent, as was the case with another former vice president, Dan Quayle.

Don't underestimate the value of perception. In the eyes of the observer, perception is reality. The observer believes that what he or she sees is real. As Norman Vincent Peale said, "It is a fact that you project what you are."

Take the case of Lloyd Adams, a successful insurance agent who specialized in deferred compensation plans for high salaried executives. After eight months of telephone calls, Lloyd finally convinced Bob Murdoch, a friend and senior vice president of a large New York City bank, to introduce him to the bank's president. The appointment was scheduled for Tuesday at 2:00 PM. Since Lloyd visited New York infrequently, he decided to have lunch at an Italian restaurant on Tuesday with an old friend.

Time flew during lunch that day. Lloyd and his friend were having a great time reliving the old days when Lloyd looked down at his watch and saw that it was 1:55 PM. He quickly settled the bill, said good-bye to his friend, and hailed a taxi for the cross-town meeting. Lloyd arrived at the bank's lobby at 2:15 PM, only to find that the receptionist wasn't there to check him in. He sat down for a few minutes and, realizing he couldn't wait any longer, walked down the hall to find Bob speaking with another man.

"Lloyd!" exclaimed Bob. "We'd given up on you. I'd like you to meet our president, Terry Rose."

"Hello, Lloyd, come on in," gestured Terry.

"I'm really sorry I'm late," blurted an apologetic Lloyd.

"That's all right," said Terry with a hint of irritation. "I have fifteen minutes before my next meeting. What was it that you had in mind?"

Recognizing that he had to cram thirty minutes of his sales pitch into fifteen, Lloyd began to quickly cover his most important points. When the time was up, Terry thanked him and said good-bye. In the days and weeks that followed, Lloyd made repeated, unsuccessful attempts to get Terry on the phone. In desperation, he called Bob. "Lloyd," said Bob, "I hate to tell you this, but Terry doesn't want to talk with you. And I hope you know why."

Yes, Lloyd did know why Terry hadn't returned his phone calls. Lloyd didn't take steps to ensure that he was early, not late. Moreover, Lloyd was in such a rush that he failed to notice two important items. One was a photo of Terry with Arnold Palmer, who happened to be one of Lloyd's clients. The other was a memento from the Young Presidents Organization given to those members who attended the university in Bombay, India. Lloyd was a YPO resource and had spoken at several YPO meetings. To make matters worse, when Lloyd took off his white shirt that night, he noticed what Terry had observed during their brief meeting—on the collar were three little red spots from the linguini with marinara sauce he'd had at lunch.

As he thought about the meeting, Lloyd realized that he had created a perception of someone who was rude, careless, and sloppy. If Terry had known about the Arnold Palmer and YPO relationships, he would add the word *inattentive*. Although this wasn't the way Lloyd was, it was Terry's perception of him. Lloyd figured that his misperception cost him in excess of $100,000 in commissions.

YOUR SELF-PERCEPTION

Ensuring that you create the correct perceptions means that you have to first decide how you want to be perceived. When people describe you, what are the adjectives you would like them to use? To get to the answer to this question, you must have a clear understanding of your brand values. These are the ideals that you bring to relationships. The values that you deem important for yourself form the perceptions you create. Take a moment to study the list of values on the table below. Rank each one "Not Important," "Somewhat Important," or "Very Important."

From this list select the six most important values in order of importance.

1. _____

2. _____

3. _____

4. _____

5. _____

6. _____

Brand Values Profile

Personal Brand Values

Value Description	Very Important	Important	Not Important	Value Description	Very Important	Important	Not Important
Accountability				Image			
Accuracy				Integrity			
Achievement				Irreverence			
Affordability				Learning			
Authenticity				Loyalty			
Balance				Nature			
Cleanliness				Nurturing			
Comfort				Optimism			
Community				Order			
Commitment				People			
Compassion				Performance			
Competition				Personal Development			
Connection				Pleasure			
Contribution				Pragmatism			
Control				Power			
Cooperation				Prestige			
Customer Intimacy				Punctuality			
Creativity				Quality			
Disclosure				Recognition			
Diversity				Reliability			
Dominance				Respect			
Economic Security				Responsibility			
Education				Responsiveness			
Empathy				Safety			
Entertainment				Security			
Fairness				Service			
Fame				Self-Motivation			
Family				Self-Respect			
Forgiveness				Simplicity			
Friendship				Sincerity			
Fun				Spirituality			
Generosity				Stability			
Golden Rule				Teamwork			
Growth				Technology			
Health				Tolerance			
Honesty				Tradition			
Humor				Trust			
Independence				Urgency			
Influence				Value			
Initiative				Variety			
Innovation				Wealth			
Intuition				Wisdom			

BRAND PROMISE

The six values that you listed are your brand values. Selecting your brand values is the easy part. How you look, act, and speak must be guided by these six ideals. If integrity is one of your values, it's imperative that every person in every relationship that you have perceives this value. Therefore, you must create and embrace a brand promise, an expression of your commitment to your values. Let's take a look at a corporate brand promise.

Prior to the introduction of the Mag-Lite® flashlight in 1979, the flashlight was generally regarded as an unreliable item that  was typically thrown away after a short time due to its inferior quality. That all changed when Anthony Maglica, founder and CEO of Mag Instrument, Inc., revolutionized the portable lighting industry. By combining superior design with reliability, durability, and an unprecedented lifetime warranty, the Mag-Lite flashlight delivers on its brand promise: A work of art that works.

The Mag-Lite Web site contains dozens of "Amazing Stories" from delighted customers who related incidents that corroborated the company's brand promise. Incredibly, one Mag-Lite flashlight went through two full cycles in a washing machine and then worked perfectly, another was merely scratched when run over by a Land Rover, a third was unscathed when lost in the snow for the entire winter, and a fourth survived for two and one-half years at the bottom of a lake.

In order to create a powerful personal brand, you, too, must create and then deliver on a brand promise. Take a few minutes to reflect on what you are willing to promise to customers, then write your promise below.

Personal Brand Promise: _____

_____

THE POWER OF 360° FEEDBACK

Your relationships will either validate or invalidate your values. How you want to be perceived and how you are perceived may be very different. You may be surprised to learn that people don't recognize your brand values or, perhaps, you are being negatively perceived. If you don't understand how you're being perceived, you will continue acting in ways that create the negative perception.

To see if you are creating the perception you desire, ask a circle of people around you who have observed you as a communicator to describe you. To obtain candid feedback, it's best to ask a friend, associate, or consultant to obtain this information. Seek out those who see you from different perspectives to fully benefit from 360° feedback. They may include:

- Your supervisor
- Peers
- Your administrative assistant
- Family members
- Vendors
- Friends
- Clients

Ask them to be open and honest. Explain that you value their feedback and will use it in your quest to become a more powerful communicator. Make their task easier by e-mailing them the Power of the Pitch 360° Feedback Form. Please see instructions on how to download this form in the Resources section.

Once you've received 360° feedback from at least six individuals, pay close attention to areas in which you received ratings of seven or less. This information provides you with a tremendous opportunity to create the perception you want.

The Power of the Pitch 360° Feedback Form

Client: Organization:

Interviewee: Organization:

Interviewer: Date:

1. What do you find most valuable about the way he/she communicates?

2. How could he/she improve his/her communication?

Rank the following elements of the presentation from 0 to 10	Excellent			Above Average			Average			Less Than Expected		
	10	9	8	7	6	5	4	3	2	1	0
Sense of Humor	☐	☐	☐	☐	☐	☐	☐	☐	☐	☐	☐
Organization	☐	☐	☐	☐	☐	☐	☐	☐	☐	☐	☐
Handouts	☐	☐	☐	☐	☐	☐	☐	☐	☐	☐	☐
Visual Aids	☐	☐	☐	☐	☐	☐	☐	☐	☐	☐	☐
Knowledge	☐	☐	☐	☐	☐	☐	☐	☐	☐	☐	☐
Listening Skills	☐	☐	☐	☐	☐	☐	☐	☐	☐	☐	☐
Rapport Developed	☐	☐	☐	☐	☐	☐	☐	☐	☐	☐	☐
Interpersonal Skills	☐	☐	☐	☐	☐	☐	☐	☐	☐	☐	☐
Presentation Skills	☐	☐	☐	☐	☐	☐	☐	☐	☐	☐	☐
Overall Rating	☐	☐	☐	☐	☐	☐	☐	☐	☐	☐	☐

Finding out the perceptions other people have of you is critical. Sometimes it even can be shocking. I know from personal experience. Before I became a communication coach, I spent about 15 years in the stockbrokerage business. One evening as I was waiting for my car outside my club, a senior club member by the name of Ken walked over to me.

"Remind me what you do, Gary" said Ken.

"I'm a stockbroker," I replied.

"Do you like being a stockbroker?" Ken asked.

"Yes, I do," I responded thoughtfully. "Why do you ask?"

"You never smile," responded Ken.

I was shocked. I could blame my dour expression on the down day in the stock market. If you're a stockbroker or significant investor, you know how devastated a market sell off can make you feel. Some days don't give you a lot to smile about, especially with the volatility of today's markets. But, Ken said, "You *never* smile." Now, I had always seen myself as a friendly, open, and happy person. *Never* smile? I felt as if he had slapped me in the face. Not only was I not smiling on that particular day, but I had never smiled at any time on any of the days of the eight years Ken and I had known each other. After I told Ken that I liked my work, Ken probably wondered why I was so sad all the time.

Ken's perception of me and my self-perception were completely opposite. Unknowingly, Ken taught me a very important life lesson that day. I must become self-aware. I wasn't aware that I didn't smile. As a child, I laughed and smiled all the time. Now, as an adult, I didn't even think about it.

EXERCISE

Once you have received the 360° feedback, compare the responses to your brand values and brand promise. Note any mismatches or inconsistencies. The awareness you gain will be invaluable as you continue to grow personally and professionally.

3

GET PSYCHED UP, NOT PSYCHED OUT

When asked what he thought about when he struck out, Babe Ruth said, "I think about hitting home runs." As in sports, a big part of making presentations is mental. Frequently we psyche ourselves out even before we get to the meeting. If we're not thinking positively about the pitch, it can go right down the drain. In this chapter, you'll see how to develop the mental attitude of a winner.

THE SPLIT PERSONALITY

If there is a mismatch between how you want to be perceived and how others perceive you, it is due to your split personality. Let's take a look at each side.

- *The Real Self.* This is the personality that your friends and family know. It's the happy, comfortable, confident person.

- *The Presentation Self.* When you are onstage, a totally different personality takes over. You may be relaxed, talking with people, maybe even joking. Now it's time for your pitch. If you were to videotape this presentation, you would see the Presentation Self. The Presentation Self might look stern, uncomfortable, even nervous. "Who is that person?" you might ask. That person is the Presentation Self.

During a workshop that we were conducting for a large construction management company, we videotaped a senior vice president giving a presentation. As we played the tape back for him, he became more and more disturbed. Finally, he threw up his arms and said, "I can't believe that I've been in my business for twenty-three years and achieved the level of success I have. With the way I come across, I'm surprised that I could persuade anyone to do anything." Although his self-evaluation may have been harsh, it does make a key point. Most of the time, people don't realize that they have split personalities.

The Presentation Self will keep you from creating the success you want. Your customers and prospects want to see the authentic person—the Real Self—and you will not persuade them unless you give them what they want. You must excise the Presentation Self.

The Presentation Self exists for several reasons. The most common is fear. According to *The Book of Lists,* the fear of public speaking is our number one fear. People would rather die, play with poisonous snakes, or jump out of airplanes than give a presentation in public. The fear is present even in the most successful entertainers. Few had the stage presence of Frank Sinatra who, cool and calm, defined charisma. Yet Sinatra confessed that, for the first four or five seconds he trembled every time he walked out on the stage. He wondered if the sound would be there when he sang the first note, if he would remember the lyrics, if his tie was right, and if he would look pleasant for the audience. After those first few seconds, the fear went away.

The feeling that we have during the first few seconds of a presentation is that same fear. At the moment of that fear, something happens to us anatomically that dates back to the time when we were cavemen and cavewomen defending our families from saber-toothed tigers. When the saber-toothed tiger charged the cave, we had two choices: fight or flight. If we chose to defend our families from the monsters, it would take tremendous amounts of energy. It would take similar energy to grab our families and outrun the tigers. The fear we experience causes our bodies to secrete the hormone adrenalin into the bloodstream to give us the energy we need.

Fast-forward several million years; the anatomic workings of our bodies haven't changed, only our perceived foes. Now the saber-toothed tiger is the audience. Perhaps you've found that the larger the audience, the greater your fear. Sometimes it's not the size but the importance of the audience. It might be just one person—the decision maker. Perhaps the saber-toothed tiger is your laptop computer, projector, or video conferencing equipment. You see, the fear that we face is much greater than the fear of public speaking; it is the fear of the unknown. *Will I forget what I'm going to say? Will I embarrass myself by not being able to answer a difficult question? Will the equipment malfunction?* With these fears comes adrenalin. The effect can be sweaty palms, shaky hands, weak knees, panic-stricken expressions, or a quivering voice.

As a result of these unpleasantries, people view adrenalin as a negative. Some even go so far as to take beta-blockers to eliminate the effects of adrenalin. This is a huge mistake. Adrenalin gives us the energy to deliver a powerful pitch. The trick is to channel the adrenalin into the positive energy that is so vital to the creation of an enthusiastic, dynamic voice, meaningful gestures, and expressive face. Now you are on your way to creating the self that people want—the real self.

Unfortunately, we are our own worst enemies. Instead of positive reinforcement, we'll crowd our minds with negative self-talk.

We'll say, "I hate giving presentations." "I'm a lousy presenter." "This is not fun." "I didn't get into this business to give presentations, and I hate it." Norman Vincent Peale said, "Believe you are defeated, believe it long enough, and it is likely to become a fact." Our negative self-talk becomes a self-fulfilling prophecy. When you blow a pitch, you say to yourself, "See, I told you I was terrible at this." Our conscious mind confirms the behavior of our subconscious mind.

Affirm

We must change this negative thinking by speaking positively to ourselves. The most effective way to do this is to create an affirmation. I used this method a number of years ago in my quest to lose weight. At five-foot-ten, I wasn't happy with the way I looked in the mirror. I weighed 168 pounds and, regardless of the diet, I could not lose weight. If you've ever attempted to lose weight, you know how frustrating the experience can be.

After many disappointing efforts, I just gave up. I had convinced myself that that's the way I was going to be. I said to myself, "I'm always going to be fat." Over time I became kinder to myself with statements like, "I'm big-boned," and, "I'm calorically challenged."

One day, at the suggestion of a friend, I decided I would end my negative self-talk. It was that day that I came up with an affirmation for myself. I wanted to lose 15 pounds, which meant that I would weigh 153 if I were successful. So my affirmation became, "I weigh 153 pounds." On that first day, I looked in the mirror in the morning and repeated my affirmation six times. That evening before I went to bed, I looked in the mirror and repeated my affirmation another six times, "I weigh 153. I weigh 153. I weigh 153. I weigh 153. I weigh 153. I weigh 153." The next day I repeated my affirmation another half a dozen times in the morning when I awoke and again in the evening when I went to bed. I continued my ritual every day without fail. I even found myself saying it to myself throughout the day.

After six months, I stood on the scale in the gym, looked down, and the numbers I had been so desperately seeking to achieve appeared: 1-5-3. Now, did I just wish and hope I would weigh 153 pounds? Not at all. I started *thinking* like a 153-pound person. I hired a personal trainer to guide me through a regular exercise program. I engaged a nutritionist to analyze my eating habits and recommend changes. It was at that moment that I understood the wisdom in Henry Ford's words, "Whether you believe you can or you believe you can't, you're right." It was my affirmation that changed my belief. Incidentally, I continue to use my affirmation. Fifteen years later, I still weigh 153 pounds.

As children, we were positive about our abilities. We even had affirmations. Like most children, my 12-year-old daughter has long been a fan of stickers. Here are some of her earlier ones.

Note that these stickers don't say, "I hate to read," "Bad reader," and "I hate books." Yet somehow over time we forget about the affirmations we cherished as children. The cruel world warps our self-confidence. "I'm not a very good presenter. I blew it the last time. I bet I'm going to blow it again."

In April 1999, I received a telephone call from Susie Whang, who asked if I would be interested in working with her daughter, Sophia, to prepare her for the California Junior Miss America Pageant in September.

"How can I help your daughter?" I asked Susie.

"Sophia is very pretty," responded Susie. "She has a 4.2 grade point average, is captain of the tennis team, plays the piano, and sings beautifully."

"Wow, she sounds like a terrific young lady, how can I help?" I asked.

"She gets very nervous and is afraid to stand on the stage and answer questions," confided Susie.

Although sixteen-year-old women with aspirations of winning pageants isn't my specialty, I agreed to work with Sophia, and we set up a schedule of coaching sessions. When Sophia entered the room at our first meeting, I saw an attractive young woman with an infectious smile. As her mother introduced us, Sophia made brief eye contact with me and gave me a limp handshake. "I am a terrible public speaker," she confided. Recognizing the challenges that we were about to face, I began our session by explaining the importance of sending positive messages to the subconscious mind.

After some discussion, I asked, "If you were to create an affirmation, what would it sound like?"

"I am a great public speaker?" asked Sophia.

"That sounds good, Sophia. Now, please write your affirmation on the flipchart," I requested. When she picked up the marker, she had difficulty writing the words as she struggled with the statement of such an obvious untruth.

Over the next three months, we worked to overcome her cultural issues about making eye contact with strangers, enhance her voice, and strengthen her presence. Every day, Sophia said her affirmation to herself many times. As the weeks passed, she became more and more confident and self-assured.

A month after our last session, I received an e-mail with the title "I am a great public speaker." I knew immediately that it was from Sophia. The message read: "I just spoke to a group of five hundred people and I was introduced by the mayor. You know, I wouldn't have ever done that before. When I finished, I received a standing ovation. I am a great public speaker."

A month later, I received a telephone call from a very excited mother. She informed me that Sophia had won the California Junior Miss Pageant. "How can I thank you, Gary?" she asked.

"Don't thank me, thank Sophia. She made it happen," I said. "She's the one who believed she was a great public speaker. All I did was point her in the right direction."

What negative self-talk do you use as you prepare for your pitch? Whatever it is, turn it around and create an affirmation. Make your affirmation brief and in the present tense. If you say to yourself, "I hate to give presentations," your affirmation might be, "I enjoy giving presentations." If you've received feedback that you lack passion, your affirmation might be, "I am a passionate speaker." Take a minute and write your affirmation in the space below.

My affirmation: _____

_____

It's important that you repeat your affirmation to yourself many times in the morning and again at night before you go to bed. By repeating your affirmation, you are sending a message from your conscious mind to your subconscious mind of how you will act. As Norman Vincent Peale said, "When you affirm big, believe big, and pray big, big things happen."

Visualize

The second step in being authentic and presenting the real self is to visualize successfully giving the presentation. See yourself connecting with the audience, smiling, and being enthusiastic. Visualize the audience interacting with you. See the key decision maker agreeing to do what you want. This visualization is a tremendous mental dry run.

Athletes use affirmations regularly, and so should we. Jack Nicklaus was a big user of visualizations. He would arrive at a golf tournament two days ahead of time. The first day he would walk around the course and take notes about the bunkers, greens, sand traps, and water hazards. The next day he'd stay in his hotel room, close the curtains, sit down, and visualize the entire game: every hole, every shot, every club.

Let's put this into context. We have established that affirmations and visualizations will help you overcome the fear of the unknown by giving you tremendous confidence. Armed with self-confidence, you will be able to show your real self. When presenting your real self to an audience, you are being authentic. It is the authentic, real self that your clients, customers, prospects, and team members want. It's so crucial that you get the mental part right. If you're unable to do so, you won't be able to maximize the value of all of the great tools and techniques in this book.

Jack Nicklaus

Source: Golf Graphics—Paul Bojanower

4

THE LAWS OF
NONVERBAL ATTRACTION

Margaret Thatcher once said, "I usually make up my mind about a man in ten seconds, and I very rarely change it." Clearly Mrs. Thatcher is in the majority because, as you learned in Chapter 1, 55 percent of total liking is based on how you look.

In this chapter, you'll learn how you can use your non-verbal gestures to define your brand and create instant likeability.

Nonverbal gestures → Attraction → Likeability

FACIAL EXPRESSION

One of the first characteristics someone will notice about you is your face. Specifically, they'll observe what type of face you have.

- *The open face.* We have 80 facial muscles capable of about seven thousand expressions. The open face shows many of

Open and Closed Face

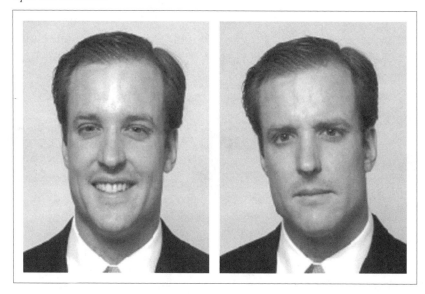

those expressions. Clients, customers, prospects, and team members want the open face.

- *The closed face.* This face has only one expression. The closed face does well in Las Vegas or Atlantic City. It's the poker face. The closed face is uninviting, distant, and unfriendly. Your audience will not be persuaded by the closed face.

The Smile

Your number one asset is your smile. When you smile at someone, you're saying, "I like you." Smiling is a key element in the Rock Star Attitude. When you smile at people in your audience, chances are they will smile back at you. When they do, they're saying, "I like you, too." Remember, people must like you before they will be persuaded by you.

Not only does your smiling have a positive impact on your audience, it can have a positive emotional effect on you. According to research conducted by Paul Ekman, University of California at San Francisco, and Richard J. Davidson, University of Wisconsin at Madison, you can cause yourself to feel happy by smiling. Believe it or not, it works. The next time you have one of those difficult days when nothing seems to go well, smile and see how much better you feel.

The failure to smile and use facial expressions is the number one challenge for our clients. They are usually so focused on what they're saying that they forget about their faces. As a result, they are perceived as closed and unfriendly, even though they are not.

Be sure your smile is genuine and sincere. Sometimes when people smile it looks painful.

On the other hand, you'll want to avoid the plastic smile that makes you look disingenuous.

Smile genuinely and appropriately when you begin your presentation, throughout your presentation, and when you conclude.

Pained, Plastic, and Sincere Smiles

Eye Connection

The fastest form of communication is eye contact. Eye contact conveys liking. When you look at a client or prospect, you're saying, "I like you." Unfortunately, many people fail to make eye contact. I'm sure you've noticed this at a cocktail reception. You may be having a conversation with a man and, as he is speaking, he is looking around the room. He may look at you occasionally, but he is not *connecting* with you. As a result of his lack of eye connection, you may feel devalued and unimportant.

When you are speaking with someone, focus your attention on that person. Look into the person's eyes and not at his or her nose, chest, or hair. Avoid the temptation to look around the room. U.S. President Ronald Reagan was excellent at making an eye connection. When you spoke with him at a reception, he focused 100 percent of his attention on you. For those few minutes you spent with him, you felt like you were the most important person in his life.

President Reagan Connecting with Me

Courtesy of Office of Ronald Reagan

This same concept of eye connection applies to the pitches you make to more than one person. The idea is to connect with each person in the room and make that person feel as if you're speaking directly to him or her. Be careful not to leave anyone out. Hold you attention on each person for two to four seconds as you move from one person to the next randomly. Don't be a lawn sprinkler with a predictable pattern.

GESTURES CREATE DRAMA

Use your hands to create powerful gestures to add emphasis to the words that you use. Think of your hands as visual aids. Make your gestures chest high so that everyone can see them. Gestures should be big, broad, and smooth. The impact will be minimal if your gestures are at your waist level.

When you're not gesturing, your hands may become a distraction if they are not playing a meaningful role in your presenta-

Gesturing Effectively and Ineffectively

tion. Avoid the temptation to place your hands in the following positions:

- *Parade Rest.* This is the military position that requires you to hold your hands behind your back when you are listening to your commander.
- *Fig Leaf.* Holding your hands in front of you is a closed position that reduces your power. Moreover, it may cause you to play with your fingers, watch, or ring, which can make you look nervous.

Parade Rest and Fig Leaf

- *Pocket Hands.* Placing your hands in your pockets is not only too casual; it makes it more difficult to use gestures. Further, you may create a huge distraction by playing with coins and keys in your pockets.
- *The Steeple.* Presenters assume this position with their hands by placing their fingers together in the form of a steeple. It serves no purpose other than being a distraction.

Pocket Hands and the Steeple

Hands at Sides

The best place for your hands when you're not gesturing is comfortably to your sides just as you do when you walk. This way your hands are out of the way and ready to gesture at the appropriate moment.

The Three-Step Power Handshake

The way you shake hands with people when you introduce yourself to them creates a powerful impression. Follow this three-step process and you'll create a positive one:

1. Make eye connection and smile.
2. As you begin your handshake, speak, "I'm John Jones. It's a pleasure to meet you."

3. Shake hands firmly while maintaining your eye connection and smile. Don't attempt to crush the person's bones, this isn't an opportunity to show someone how strong you are. The fleshy part of your hand between your thumb and forefinger must touch the same area of the hand you are shaking.

Above all, never give someone the Limp Fish handshake. This rule applies equally to both sexes. In the 19th century, men introduced themselves to women by gently gripping the palm and top of the hand. There is no need for such differentiation today.

Power Handshake and the Limp Fish

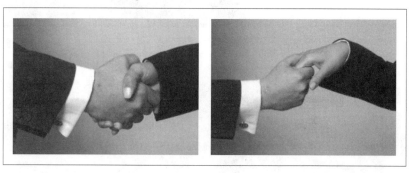

AVOID DISTRACTING MANNERISMS

Distracting mannerisms are actions that you repeat that cause people to focus more on the mannerisms than on what you're saying. Some of the most common include:

- Adjusting your glasses
- Moving your hair out of your face
- Adjusting your tie
- Touching your face
- Playing with or holding a pen, pencil, or marker

Some people have their own unique mannerisms, as did a man I observed several years ago. Every time he wanted to emphasize a significant point, he raised his right eyebrow. I became so fixated with his eyebrow raising that I lost his message.

If you have distracting mannerisms, you may not know it. One of the best ways to gain awareness is to videotape yourself in a role-play giving a pitch to a prospect. Then play the videotape back and pay close attention to what you do with your hands and your face.

POSTURE

Sitting

If you're sitting, sit up, forward, and engaged. You will create an energetic, dynamic feel with this position. Keep your hands on top of and not under the table. This is one of the first rules of broadcasting—you don't want the audience wondering what you're doing with you hands. The same applies to making a pitch. Importantly, resting your hands on the table allows you to use gestures easily.

Correct Sitting Position

Standing

Whenever possible, stand to make a pitch; it gives you more authority. For the most part, deciding whether to stand or sit is a consideration of the size of the audience. As a rule of thumb, stand when you present to more than three people. Stand tall with your shoulders back. A good way to check your posture is to stand with your back against the wall. You may be surprised at how you slouch. The

Correct and Incorrect Stance

position of your feet also is important. If your feet are far apart, you will rock side to side as you shift your weight from one foot to the other. For those who are focusing on you, this could be like watching a tennis match. To prevent yourself from rocking, bring your feet close together, almost touching.

THE PRINCIPLE OF CLOSE PROXIMITY

This principle says that we get close to people we like and distance ourselves from people we don't like. Remembering the Rock Star Attitude, you want to show people that you like them by being as close to them as possible without invading their space.

Unfortunately, your prospects and clients will make it difficult for you if you leave the seating arrangements to them. Typically, people will sit at the opposite end of a conference table or at the back of the room.

Instead of leaving it up to the audience, seat clients and prospects as close to you as possible, as in Figure 4.11. Note your position at the end of the table. This allows you to make an eye connection with the people to your right and left. When you show

Correct Room Setup

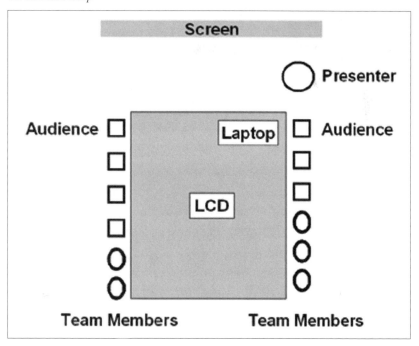

The Barrier

slides on the screen, move either to the right or the left, ensuring that you're not blocking the audience's view. For team presentations, seat your team members at the back of the table. When it's time for them to present, they move to the front of the room to the position you previously held.

The Principle of Close Proximity applies equally to larger audiences (e.g., employee, city council, and town hall meetings). Instead of a conference table, your audience may be seated in a classroom or theater style. Nonetheless, you want to be as close to people as you can be without invading their space. This means avoiding lecterns whenever possible. Although it may be more comfortable to present from behind a lectern, it serves as a barrier between you and the audience. Instead of a lectern, place a small table for your notes close to the audience.

MOVEMENT

Movement provides action within the room and takes the energy level up. Of course, you want to be sure you move with purpose and that you're not pacing back and forth. As in the following diagram, position number one is in the center of the room. Position number two is to your right, and position number three is to your left. In a larger room, there could be more positions. At each position, make eye connection with everyone in the room, not just at the people seated in front of you.

One of the best examples of how to use the Principle of Close Proximity was when Elizabeth Dole spoke at the 1996 Republican Convention in an effort to persuade the delegates to nominate

Movement Positions

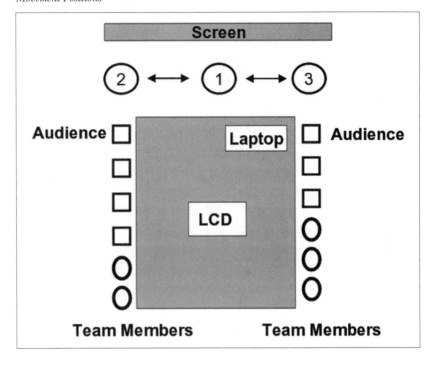

her husband, Bob Dole. Every other speaker addressed the delegates from a podium some distance from the audience. Mrs. Dole, however, left the podium, walked down into the audience, and spoke from a number of positions on the convention floor. At one point she placed her hand on the shoulder of a disabled man as she talked about her husband's dedication to assisting disabled Americans. Not only was this a powerful presentation, it brought Mrs. Dole further into the national spotlight and paved the way for her successful bid for the U. S. Senate seat for North Carolina.

EXERCISE

Videotape yourself giving a typical customer or prospect pitch. Then, play the video back, paying close attention to the following:

- *Your brand values.* Does your image convey these values?
- *The 360° feedback from people who have seen you make a pitch.* Can you validate their perceptions?
- *The chapter lessons.* Are you applying the lessons you learned in this chapter?

5

THE POWER OF PACKAGING

Think of yourself as a present you are going to give to a customer or prospect. What do you want your package to look like? You could wrap yourself in plain brown paper and twine. Or you could select colorful paper, beautiful ribbon and an attractive bow. If prospective customers find your package unattractive or inappropriate, they won't be interested in it unless you can convince them that what's inside the package is so valuable that they should overlook the package. This is a big hurdle to overcome and one you need not face. If given the choice between your dull package and a beautiful package that contains equal value, they will select the attractive one. The way you package yourself is a defining component of your brand and an important factor people will measure in determining if they like the way you look. Your packaging consists of your wardrobe, accessories, and grooming. Here, you'll learn how to make your packaging an asset in winning more business.

DRESS TO YOUR SUCCESS

Notice that the title of this section is "Dress *to* Your Success" and not "Dress *for* Success." The key word change from *for* to *to* was suggested to me by one of our clients, former college basketball coach Jim Harrick. I worked with Jim on a series of keynote speeches he was to deliver soon after he had just taken UCLA to the NCAA Basketball National Championship in 1995.

"When I took over as head coach," said Jim, "the team would go on trips in sweat pants, sweat shirts, denim, or some combination thereof. They looked like a bunch of college kids. So I had a talk with them one day. I said, 'Fellas, when we're in the public, people are watching us every minute. How we come across is very important. We need to look like winners. Let me ask you a question. When you leave UCLA, what do you want to do?'

Coach Jim Harrick

"Of course, most of them said they wanted to play in the pros. Some wanted to be coaches and television commentators," continued Jim. "So I asked them, 'How do those people dress?' Well, the change was unbelievable," Jim chuckled. "On our next trip, the guys were wearing sharp suits, nice ties, and good looking shoes. From that point on, we stopped looking like a high school team and started looking like a top rated collegiate team."

The idea is to dress to the level of success that you want to achieve in the future, not where you were in the past. Many times people still dress the way they did earlier in their careers. Think about where you want to be in the future and dress to that level. The way you dress defines your brand image just as much as the nonverbal gestures we discuss in Chapter 4.

THE ONE-NOTCH PRINCIPLE

Always dress slightly better than the best-dressed person in your audience. Implicit in the One-Notch Principle is that you don't dress down, you dress up. If prospects are casually dressed in pants and shirts, one notch means that you might add a blazer to your ensemble. If women are wearing blazers and men jackets and ties, you wear a suit. Of course, if clients are wearing suits, you, too, should wear a suit.

The One-Notch Principle will prevent you from dressing so far above the level of your audience that there is a disconnect. Some companies, particularly in the entertainment and computer software industries, frown on wearing business suits. The solution is simple; always ask the prospect, client, or meeting planner ahead of time.

If you typically wear a business suit and one afternoon you decide to tour one of your plants, construction sites, or a similar environment, consider changing to casual clothes ahead of time. At a minimum, take off your suit jacket and roll up your sleeves. If you're a man, loosen you tie.

The one exception to the One-Notch Principle is if there is an expectation that you dress in a certain manner. Even though many companies have switched to business casual, you may be asked to wear business attire for a presentation.

An investment advisory firm was asked to make a pitch to manage some of the funds in the Hawaii State Employees Retirement System. Since the presentation was in Hawaii, the investment advisory team decided to wear Aloha shirts. To show team unity, each team member purchased the identical red and blue flowery shirt. At the presentation, the investment advisory team was surprised that the selection committee members were dressed in sports coats and ties. One of the investment advisory team members confided in me, "Gary, I've never felt like more of an idiot." Moreover, each of the three other investment advisory firms that also made presentations wore suits and ties. Correctly, they dressed one notch above the prospect, while our Aloha friends were several notches below.

NOTHING SHOULD DISTRACT

Nothing about the way you look—your clothing, hygiene, or grooming—should distract. Once people notice the distraction, you run the risk that they will focus on that and not your presentation.

A television commercial provides an excellent example of how devastating a distraction can be. The scene opens with an executive in a business suit walking briskly down the hall en route to an important meeting, portfolio in his right hand. He is met by a teammate who wishes him good luck and then radios ahead to another teammate to remove toilet paper from one of the executive's shoes. As the second teammate makes the adjustment, he wishes the executive good luck and radios the next teammate about static cling. The third teammate pulls the executives right pant leg down to cover his shoe, wishes him good luck and radios the next teammate to remove dandruff from the executive's suit coat. The fourth teammates wishes the executive good luck and whisks the dandruff from the shoulder of the executive's suit. Finally, the executive arrives at the lobby where he meets a group of Japanese executives.

"Gentlemen," he says as he greets his guests, "glad to meet you." The executive then smiles broadly, exposing a piece of lettuce on his teeth.

His team remedied all the distractions he should have noticed, except one. Can you imagine watching someone with lettuce stuck in his teeth speak to you for an hour? Once a prospect notices such a distraction, it will be difficult for her to concentrate on your message. Your pitch will be over before it even starts.

THE THREE Ts

The Three Ts will provide you with conservative guidelines for selecting the clothing that you will wear to the pitch. Keep in mind that these are guidelines and that you must be aware of what is acceptable in your profession. If you are in a creative role, for instance, in the entertainment or advertising industry, you may take a more casual approach than an executive in the accounting or legal profession.

Traditional

Traditional clothing is accepted in any presentation venue. These are the more conservative styles worn by most business professionals. This is not high fashion. In fact, a survey of executives found that these executives would not hire someone that came to the interview dressed in high fashion. Not only did the executives find high fashion distracting, they felt that people who spent so much time on their clothing would be too self-focused. Another plus for traditional clothing is that it goes out of style slowly, thus giving you much longer wear.

Tasteful

Nothing will be more offensive or distracting than gaudy clothing. Clothing should be made of natural fibers or natural-looking fibers. Dark colors, such as navy blue, dark gray, and black, signify

Traditional and Tasteful

Photo by Melinda Kelley

authority for either gender, but women can wear more colors then men. Royal blue, emerald green, and deep purple imply confidence.

Lighter colors such as light blue or light gray express calm and organization. Earth tones create a feeling of warmth. If you want to come across in a warm, friendly, nonauthoritarian way, these colors are a good choice. Notice how many white-collar criminal attorneys will have their clients wear earth tone suits and monochromatic ties. An attorney wants the jury to look at their client and ask, "How could he possibly have done that? He doesn't look the part."

Tailored

Be sure your clothing fits you well. Ill-fitting clothing is not only distracting, it sends a message that you're not paying atten-

Earth Tones

Photo by Melinda Kelley

tion to details. Be sure the length of your jacket sleeves and your pants is appropriate. If you've gained or lost weight, have your clothing adjusted.

Women will want to be especially careful to send the appropriate message by avoiding styles that are too tight or that expose too much skin. Also, check that a front or side skirt slit doesn't rise inappropriately high when you're seated.

Button your jacket whenever you stand up. Not only does this create a more professional silhouette, it keeps your shirt or blouse from poofing out. As a sign of respect, put your jacket on when a client who is wearing a jacket visits you in your office.

SHIRTS AND BLOUSES

Shirts and blouses should be made of natural fibers, such as cotton and silk, or look like they are. The greater the contrast between the shirt or blouse and the jacket, the greater the authority. The maximum authority is a white blouse or shirt with a dark suit jacket or coat.

As you change the color of the shirt or blouse, for example, to light blue to ecru to pink, you reduce the authority and formality. The same is true for dark-colored shirts and blouses.

The rule in stripes is the narrower the stripe and the closer together the stripes, the greater the authority. For men, have your shirts medium starched to add a crisp look.

For women, wear a camisole under a sheer blouse, and make sure that any knit top you may choose to wear under a suit jacket isn't too tight, thin, or casual. For men, since you can see through most men's dress shirts always wear a crew neck—not a V-neck or tank top—undershirt. You never want the audience to see you sweat.

A Wild Tie

TIES

This is the one part of a man's wardrobe that he can use to create some individuality. But, be careful, as ties also can act as distractors—you don't want someone studying the golf scene on your tie and not paying attention to your message. Save the fun Nicole Miller or Jerry Garcia ties for social events.

For business, think conservative. The rule is the smaller the pattern or the narrower the stripes, the more conservative the tie. In many cases, quality, conservative ties add an air of sophistication.

Be sure your tie is straight and snug against your collar. Wearing your tie a half-mast will create the appearance of carelessness.

Tie Snug and at Half-Mast

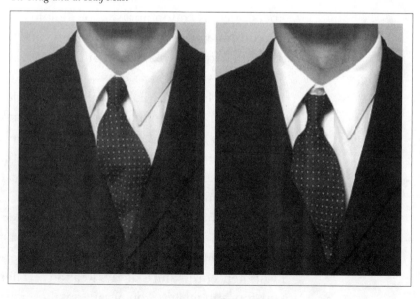

Conservative Jewelry

JEWELRY

The key idea is less is more. Select a few pieces of high-quality jewelry. As a rule of thumb, limit rings to one per hand. For women, jangling bracelets and swaying earrings can be distracting. For men, bracelets are inappropriate for any conservative business environment.

Choose a small-faced watch and leave the sports watch for the weekend.

Conservative Watch and Sports Watch

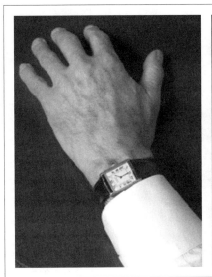 

SHOES

Your shoes complete the package and say something about your understanding of fashion and attention to detail. Always, always keep them shined and in good condition.

For Men

Start by purchasing good quality shoes that are appropriate for the clothing you will wear to the pitch. If you're wearing a suit, select lace-up shoes for the most conservative look. Lace-ups can be plain-toed, cap-toed, or wing-tipped. Be sure they are dress shoes, not thick rubber–soled walking shoes. A more casual option is tassel or buckle loafers. Never wear penny loafers with a suit, since this combination creates a mismatch. If you're wearing a sport coat with or without a tie, select tassel or buckle loafers.

Shined Shoes

Never wear formal lace-up shoes when you wear a sport coat—this also matches styles that don't work together. If you're dressing business casual (i.e., without a jacket), select tassel, buckled, or penny loafers. Do not wear lace-ups for this combination, either.

Base the color of your shoes on the color of your pants. If your pants are black, navy blue, gray, or olive, select black shoes. Cordovan is an option for navy blue and gray. If your pants are brown, select brown or cordovan. If your pants are tan, tan shoes are the best choice.

For Women

If you're wearing a suit, select closed-toe and heel pumps with heels of one to two inches. Avoid stilettos or mules.

Although many of the same rules for men apply to women as well, women have many more options than men. If you choose to wear a black, navy blue, or dark gray suit, black pumps are a good choice. With lighter-colored suits, select a shoe color the same shade or darker than the hem of the garment. White shoes, prints, or excessive ornamentation attract attention to your feet and should, therefore, be avoided—you want people to look at your face, not your feet.

HOSIERY

For Women

For business, the conservative choice is sheer panty hose or nylons with dresses and skirts. Save textured and opaque, colored panty hose for a business casual environment. Knee-highs that match the pants or shoes are a good choice. Always wear hose with a dress or skirt.

Exposed Skin

For Men

Men's hosiery should be over the calf. If you wear regular length socks, your pant leg will ride up your leg when you sit down. This will produce an unpleasant distraction.

One of my friends, John Voss, told me about a meeting he had with former California Governor, Pat Brown. "The governor greeted my business partner and me and invited us to sit down on the chairs in front of his desk," recounted John. "He then sat down in a chair behind his desk, leaned back, and put his feet up on his desk. As he did, his pant leg came up about half-way between his shoe and his knee, and he had on a pair of these thin, black nylon anklet socks," said John. "Now, this was a very important meeting. My partner and I were there to present a business deal. But, all I can recall about that day is this patch of white, hairy leg. That's my remembrance of the governor."

Also, the color of your socks should match the color of your pants. If you're wearing navy blue pants, wear navy blue socks. With black pants select black socks, and with gray pants choose gray or black socks.

ACCESSORIES

There are many ways to accessorize your wardrobe. If you're a man, you might choose to wear a handkerchief neatly folded and placed in the lapel pocket of your suit.

Accessories

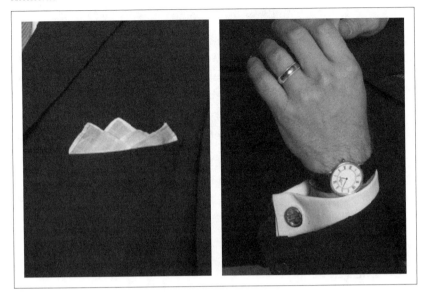

Cufflinks are another option for men and women. However, in some industries such as construction and engineering, they may be seen as pretentious. Others, such as law and commercial real estate, might view cuff links as a status symbol.

Be sure that your purse, portfolio, briefcase, belt, pen, or wallet are consistent with the quality of your wardrobe. A canvas bag from your last convention or the plastic pen you took from your hotel room sends a mixed message about your image. Be sure to color coordinate your belt with your shoes.

GROOMING

Pay close attention to grooming. Get a haircut before you need one. Be sure to wash and style your hair the morning of the pitch. Keep your fingernails clean and neatly trimmed. Step into the restroom before your presentation to ensure that your hair is combed, your clothing is properly adjusted, and, for women, your makeup isn't smeared.

Because women have more options in this department as well, they also have more grooming rules. For the pitch, conservative, neutral-colored makeup gives a polished, appropriate look. Avoid extra long fingernails or ornaments placed on your nails—a French manicure or subtle polish is the least distracting. Colored hair should be refreshed and roots should not be obvious.

For both men and women, a subtle fragrance goes a long way. Be sure you pass the Whisper Test: people should not be able to smell your perfume, cologne, or aftershave unless they whisper something in your ear.

CONSISTENCY

Remember that you're always on stage. People will observe you long after the presentation is over. Be sure that your image is consistent.

One of our clients, a managing partner of a large law firm, confirmed the importance of this principle. "A few years ago," said the managing partner, "we had outgrown our space and needed to expand to nearly double our then one hundred thousand-square-foot office space. So, we sent out Requests for Proposals and set up interviews with five commercial real estate firms that specialized in tenant representation.

"The last of the five firms," continued the partner, "was represented by two very sharp brokers. They discussed how they could expertly meet our needs in a professional manner. At the end of their presentation, one of the men asked, 'Can you see how we are the firm to help you with this important relocation of your offices?' I replied, "Yes, I can, but give us a day to discuss it further. I can tell you, though, that I'm almost certain we will give you the business.'

"With that, they thanked us, said they would follow up in a day, and left," said the managing partner. "I walked back to my office and looked out the window at the parking lot below, contemplating the busy day we had just had. Just then, I saw the two brokers walking through the parking lot headed for their car. As they walked along, I noticed that they were laughing. I asked myself; I wonder what they're laughing at? I wonder if they're laughing about us? I wonder if they're laughing about me? As they got to their car, they turned to each other and gave each other a big high five. They then got into their car and drove away.

"Well, I reported this scene at the partners meeting the next morning," concluded the managing partner, "and one senior partner became so irate that he insisted that we dismiss the commercial real estate firm and these two brokers from further consideration. By not realizing they were still on stage when they walked through the parking lot, they lost about two million dollars in commissions."

Don't talk about the presentation you just made until you're back in your office with the door closed. You never know who might be listening or watching. Life is one big stage. Be sure that your packaging and the way you present it are consistent as you move from one stage to another.

6

PUT POWER
IN YOUR VOICE

Have you ever listened to presenters who looked great but when they spoke, you were shocked by their weak voices? Perhaps they spoke in monotones, screeched in a high pitch, were so quiet you couldn't hear them, or so fast you couldn't understand. Let's be sure you're not that kind of presenter.

Once people like how you look, they will pay attention to how you sound. If they don't like how you sound, they may stop listening, regardless of your message. If they tune you out, it doesn't matter what you say, you're not going to persuade them to do anything. In this chapter, we will look at the vocal qualities you must possess in order keep people interested in your presentations. You'll also learn some specific words to use to move people to action.

BE ENTHUSIASTIC

Walter Chrysler had it right when he said, "The real secret of success is enthusiasm." If you're enthusiastic, your audience will be, too. Steve Balmer, the president of Microsoft, is wildly enthusiastic about his company. He kicked off a recent annual employee meeting by running on to the stage to an upbeat song and yelling, "Get up! Get up!" People stood as he danced around the stage. Panting and out of breath, he approached the microphone and said, "I have four words for you. I . . . love . . . this . . . company!" He opens every employee annual meeting this way. He may be over the top, but no one at Microsoft doubts his passion.

In sharp contrast, many presenters give their presentations in the same somber mood that a newscaster might if she were announcing the downing of a commercial jetliner with two hundred people aboard. Don't be one of those presenters. If you're not enthusiastic, your audience won't be. The audience won't care that you just flew in from Singapore, are suffering from indigestion, or have given the same pitch every day for the last month. People want you to create an upbeat, enjoyable experience for them.

Take a minute to complete the following sentence:

My favorite day of the year is _____.

Go ahead, write it down. You may have answered *my birthday, New Year's Day, the first day of daylight savings, my anniversary, the first day of football season,* or another day that is very special to you. How do you feel on that special day? Happy? Excited? Upbeat? That's the same feeling that you want to bring to a presentation. You want clients and prospects to ask, "Is today your birthday?" "Is it New Year's Day?" "Is it the first day of football season?" If all other elements of the pitch, such as experience, knowledge, and cost, are equal, enthusiasm will win the business.

Don't save your enthusiasm just for the presentations. Be enthusiastic throughout the day, from the first person you greet in the morning. I'm surprised at some of the dreary responses I receive when I greet people. I'll usually use a cheerful "Good morning!" Some of the responses I receive range from a barely audible "Mornin'" to a disillusioned "What's so good about it?" By greeting people enthusiastically, you not only are working to ensure your enthusiasm is consistent, you will have a positive impact on you feelings.

Frequently, I'll ask, "How are you doing?" The answers to this question usually vary between "Not bad," "Fair," and "Fine." How can you go from one of these dull responses to being enthusiastic in a presentation? You can't! Instead, reply with a "Terrific," "Excellent," "Great," or "Fabulous." Even when you're not feeling all that great, enthusiastic responses stated by your conscious mind will have a positive impact on your subconscious. Yes, you can change how you feel.

VOICE DYNAMICS

A dynamic voice possesses four key elements. Let's take a look at each.

Projection

You want to be sure that you speak loud enough so everyone in the room can easily hear what you're saying. You must dominate the room, not vice versa. That means the sounds you make need to come from your diaphragm, the muscle located just below your rib cage. Speaking from the diaphragm forces the air up and out of your lungs and out of your mouth. If you use your throat muscles to force air out of your mouth, you will become hoarse.

Inflection

Varying the tones of your voice creates inflection. When there is no variation, you speak in monotone. Raising and lowering the tones of your voice adds emphasis to key points. In the statement, "We will save you five million dollars," raising the tones on "five million dollars" emphasizes the most important words

Range

You produce range in your voice by raising and lowering the volume. Raising the volume allows you to emphasize key words. By raising the volume on "five million dollars," you will emphasize the significance of this amount of money. Conversely, lowering the volume to a whisper will emphasize key words, too.

Pace

Pace is how quickly or how slowly you speak. We speak at approximately 120 to 140 words a minute. John Moshitta, who became known for the lightening speed at which he spoke in the Federal Express commercials during the 1980s, holds the world record at a blazing 586 words per minute. If you speak too fast, people may understand you, but they won't be able to distinguish what's important.

Similarly, if you speak too slowly, you won't be able to emphasize key words. Pacing works best when you speed up through areas that aren't so important or difficult to understand and slow down through areas that are more important or difficult.

As you pace yourself, remember to use the pause, an important and underutilized tool. Whenever you pause, what you say right after the pause takes on heightened emphasis. "We will save

you . . . five million dollars." Be careful not to use so many pauses
that your speech pattern is halting, but do pause frequently to un-
derscore key words or phrases.

A long pause that creates silence is powerful. Don't feel like
you have to be talking all the time. This is not radio. We don't
have to worry about dead air. Perhaps you know the expression
from negotiation, "The first person to speak loses." If you're
going for the close, ask the question, "Can you see us working on
your behalf?" Then don't say anything. All too frequently we are
tempted to say something else to break the silence. "Well, maybe
the timing's not right." "If the fee is too high, we might be able to

Projection, Range, Inflection, and Pace

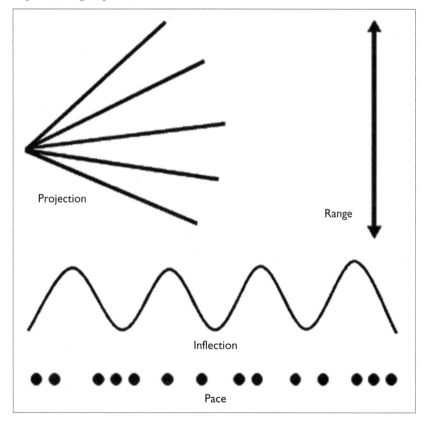

Projection

Range

Inflection

Pace

reduce it for you." Just be quiet and look calmly at the prospect. Let the prospect speak first. Who knows? He or she might say, "Yes."

The misuse of pace can cause presentation anxiety, which occurs when you've prepared and rehearsed a pitch so well that you just can't wait to deliver it. Finally, the time you've been waiting for arrives. It's show time, and away you go! *No, don't stop me. Don't slow me down. No, you can't buy now. You have to let me get through my entire presentation.* What happens if you're giving a presentation and the buyer, five minutes into the presentation, says, "I've got it. Great idea. Let's do it!"? What happens to the presentation you spent five hours on? Dump it in the trashcan and say to the prospect, "Terrific. Sign right here." Don't keep talking after someone says he's ready to buy. If you do, you might talk him out of the sale.

When you engage the four elements of the voice dynamics—projection, inflection, range, and pace—and couple them with a strong image, you have the opportunity to win people over. One of the best examples in recent history of someone who perfected the use of voice dynamics is Bill Clinton. The world first learned about his tremendous oratory skills during the three U.S. presidential debates with George Bush and Ross Perot in October 1992.

It was the second debate at the University of Richmond that separated Bill Clinton from his opponents. While George Bush and Ross Perot either sat on or stood beside their respective stools, Bill Clinton moved to the audience, where he connected with people as he spoke in a personal, persuasive, yet energetic manner. Within months, it became clear the we had found a successor to Ronald Reagan, as the "Great Communicator."

SPEAK POSITIVELY

Frequently, we use words that are not negative, but at the same time they're not positive, either. I call them non-positive words. Here are some examples.

Problem

When you use the word *problem* it indicates an order of magnitude much greater than reality, as in, "We have a real problem." The word *problem* creates a sense of hopelessness. "What are we going to do about the problem?" Instead of the word *problem*, use words such as *challenge, situation,* or *issue.*

No Problem

As with the word *problem,* the words *no problem* place a negative spin on the message. We hear *no problem* used in many service establishments. You ask a waiter to bring you some more bread. When he places the bread on the table in front of you, you say, "Thank you," to which he replies, "No problem." Well, of course it's not a problem. Providing a service in a service establishment where patrons pay for that service is not a problem. Why even hint that there might be a problem? The correct mindset is for servers to understand that providing a service is an honor. The next time you're at a Four Seasons Hotel, note what a server says in return for your thanks. It will never be *no problem.* Instead, he will say, "You're welcome" or "It's my pleasure."

Try

People don't want you to try. I dropped off my car at an auto repair shop not long ago. I asked the attendant if I could get my car by 5:00 PM. since I didn't have another way to get home. He said to me, "We'll try to have it ready for you by 5:00." Try wasn't good enough, I needed my car.

Take a tip from Yoda in *Star Wars*. When Luke Skywalker found it impossible to move a large stone, Yoda urged him to call on his mental strength to perform the Herculean task.

Luke Skywalker: All right, I'll give it a try.
Yoda: No. Try not. Do . . . or do not. There is no "try."

Don't say, "What we try to do for clients is provide them with excellent service." Implicit in the word *try* is an element of doubt. It signals to prospects that you may not be successful in providing excellent service. Instead say, "What we do for clients. . . ."

Want, Can

Don't tell prospects or customers what you *want* to do or *can* do for them if they buy your products or services. As an example, if you're a stockbroker, don't say to a prospect, "What we *want* to do is to structure a diversified portfolio of quality stocks." Replace the *want* with *will*. "What we *will* do is to structure a diversified portfolio of quality stocks." *Want* represents your desire or intent. *Will* defines a definite action. *Can* means that you are able, as in, "What we *can* do for you." As with *want*, replace this non-positive word with *will*.

Kind of, Sort of

Remove these weak words when you describe an action you will take for people. Instead of "We will *sort of* work together as teams," say "We *will* work together as teams."

Hopefully, Probably, Maybe

These words weaken your presentation and raise doubt as to the validity of your statements. "Hopefully, we have come up with a great solution for you." "Probably you'll see that our team is very talented." "Maybe you'll get tremendous benefit from our service." Eliminate these non-positives and just say it. "We have a very talented team." "You'll get tremendous benefit from our service." Be positive.

Think, Believe, Feel, In My Opinion

These are the all-time great qualifiers. "I believe that we have a great product." When you add the word *believe,* you qualify your statement. The message is, "This is what I believe, but I could be wrong. Our product may not be that great. In fact, you'd better compare our product carefully with the competition's to be sure." These qualifiers minimize the impact of your statement on the audience. Again, just say it. "We have a great product."

One of the most positive orators in history was the Rev. Dr. Martin Luther King. During a supercharged five-day riot in April 1968, in Birmingham, Alabama, twenty-five hundred African Americans were jailed. It was a socially unjust time in the United States. At the end of those five days, Dr. King spoke to the nation.

I just want to do God's will. And he's allowed me to go up to the mountain. And I've looked over and I've seen the promise land. I may not get there with you, but I want you to know tonight that we as a people will get to the promise land.

"We as a people *will* get to the promise land." Dr. King understood the power of positive words. Despite the horrific treatment and uncertain future of African Americans, he left no doubt as to his determination to seek justice. He spoke positively in every speech he gave, including this prophetic last one, which he delivered one day before he was gunned down in Memphis, Tennessee. In addition to his considerable accomplishments, Dr. King taught us an important lesson of just how powerful speaking positively can be.

OBSERVE THE RULES OF GRAMMAR

You may not think much about grammar, but it is just as much of a part of your brand as the clothes you wear. Polished grammar will improve any impression you will make. Still, common grammatical errors do sneak into the most prepared presentations. A must-have resource is Strunk and White's 92-page book *The Elements of Style.* You'll find this tool an invaluable reference.

Here are a few rules to keep in mind.

Incorrect Pronouns

Me and John. As in, "Me and John did it." The correct form of the pronoun is nominative, *I,* and not objective, *me,* because both John and the speaker are the subjects of the verb. Also, personal pronouns always follow in a conjunction. Therefore, the correct phrasing is, "John and I did it."

Great, and yourself? This is the response someone will give you when you greet him or her. As in, "How are you?" "Great, and yourself?" The word *yourself* is reflective. It is intended to reflect back in the sentence to another pronoun, as in "I did it myself." The correct word is *you,* as in, "Great, and you?"

The Passive Voice

The active voice is more dynamic and direct than the passive voice.

Passive voice: *Our recommendations on how we can assist you will be presented at our next meeting by us.*

In an effort to make the passive voice seem less awkward, a presenter might omit the *by us,* though that merely makes the statement indefinite.

Active voice: *At our next meeting we will present our recommendations on how we can assist you.*

Redundancies

Many times, we combine two words that have the same or similar meanings. In the following examples, use one of the words, but not both.

- First and foremost
- Each and every
- If and when
- Pure and simple
- Short and sweet
- Unless and until

Unnecessary Modifiers

Similarly, we use superfluous adjectives and adjectives.

Incorrect	**Correct**
Forgone conclusion	Conclusion
I will go ahead and do it	I will do it
The foreseeable future	The future

Pronunciation

The audience may forgive you if you mispronounce a word, but do it several times in your presentation, and people will perceive you as uneducated. Here is a sampling of words commonly mispronounced.

Incorrect	Correct
Athelete	Athlete
Axe	Ask
Expresso	Espresso
Febuary	February
Forte	Fort. Although the word is spelled forte, pronounce the [e] as an [a] only when speaking of music
Hunderd	Hundred
Irregardless	Regardless
Jewlery	Jewelry
Libary	Library
Pitcher	Picture
Pronounciation	Pronunciation
Realitor	Realtor
Tiajuana	Tijuana
Triathalon	Triathlon
Verbage	Verbiage
Vica-versa	Vice-versa

Avoid Fillers

Fillers are words and noises we use to fill space in a sentence while we think of what we're going to say. The most common fillers include:

Uh	Like
Um	And
OK	But
Well	So
You know	Now

Not only are fillers annoying, they reduce the power of your message. To rid yourself of these pesky verbal distractions, pause every time you sense a filler coming on. Then, work on eliminating the pauses.

ARTICULATION

Articulation won't ensure that your presentation will be a winner, but it will add polish. We have become very lazy in that we don't enunciate the syllables in words. As a result, we have developed poor speaking habits. We start by dropping the "g" at the end of words. Then it escalates:

Incorrect	Correct
havin'	Having
goin'	Going
gunna	Going to
hafta	Have to
Whatcha gunna do?	What are you going to do?
Becuz, cuz	Because

THINK WORD ECONOMY

Frequently, we crowd our messages with too many words. An excellent exercise is to transcribe your presentation. You'll be shocked at how many excess words you use.

Here are some examples of verbose expressions and their replacements:

Verbose	Brief
With regard to	Regarding
This point in time	Now
Due to the fact that	Because
Is not in a position to	Can't
Once in a great while	Occasionally
Come to a decision	Decide
Take into consideration	Consider
As a matter of fact	Just say it. Instead of "As a matter of fact, it's sunny today," just say, "It's sunny today."
Take the position that	Just say it.
To be perfectly honest	So, you've been lying all along. Now you're going to be honest. Just say it.
To be perfectly candid	
Honestly	
To tell you the truth	
Let me be frank	

CUT CLICHÉS

Clichés are overused expressions that we come to rely on as a lazy of way of expressing ourselves. You may know that "cliché" is a French word that means "old picture." Instead of using these tired old pictures, come up with new, fresh expressions. Here are some common examples of clichés:

- Add insult to injury
- An honor and a privilege

- At the end of the day
- Bite the bullet
- Burn your bridges
- Easier said than done
- Grain of salt
- Handwriting on the wall
- Have a nice day
- Hit the nail on the head
- Heads up
- Ignorance is bliss
- If the shoe fits
- In one ear and out the other
- It goes without saying
- Keep a stiff upper lip
- Keep your eye on the ball
- Last but not least
- Let's touch base
- Moment of truth
- More than she bargained for
- Needs no introduction
- Net-net
- Never a dull moment
- No brainer
- On the same page
- Out of sight, out of mind
- Play it by ear
- Put my foot down
- Put the cart before the horse
- Roll out the red carpet
- Round of applause
- Quick and dirty
- Share some thoughts
- Six of one and a half-dozen of the other
- Slam-dunk

- Stiff upper lip
- The bottom line
- The heavy lifting
- The low-hanging fruit
- The rock of Gibraltar
- The 30,000 feet view
- Think out of the box
- Through thick and thin
- Throw in the towel
- To make a long story short
- Tough act to follow
- Unable to see the forest for the trees
- Water under the bridge
- When it's all said and done

Similarly, you may have clichés in your business or profession. Those expressions are fine when you talk with others in your field, but can be confusing to prospects and clients who may be unfamiliar with these specialized terms. Play it safe, speak in comprehensible expressions.

PRACTICE MAKES PERMANENT

Read Aloud Daily

A number of years ago, I took a 14-week voiceover workshop to prepare me for some audio programs I was going to record. At the end of the first session, our instructor gave us some commercial copy and said, "Go home and read aloud every night for five minutes." I thought to myself, "I'm a professional speaker. I don't need to do this." So, I skipped the assignment.

The next week when my fellow students went into the sound booth to read copy and receive coaching from the instructor, I noticed everyone was a little bit better than they were the previous week. As for me, I struggled with the lines I had to read. I found it difficult to give the special meaning to the words our teacher wanted. At end of the session, she reminded us, "Don't forget, read aloud five minutes every day." Continuing to feel like this was a silly exercise, I didn't practice the second week, either.

The following week, as I continued to be challenged by reading new copy in the sound booth, and as the 12 other students watched, the teacher stopped me. "Gary," she asked politely, "have you been reading aloud every day?" I looked at her with a sheepish grin and replied, "No." She paused for a few seconds and said, "I can tell."

After I regained my composure, I pledged to master reading aloud. The impact that this simple exercise had on me during the remainder of the voiceover workshop was profound.

When you think about it, reading aloud makes sense. If you exercise, you may walk, run, bicycle, or go to the gym. You exercise your muscles much more than you would by working at your desk. Yet we never exercise our communication muscles—our mouth, lips, and tongue—for the sake of exercise. We just use them and expect to perform flawlessly. Be sure you give these muscles a workout, too.

The two-minute drill. If your presentation is early in the morning, warm your vocal muscles up with a the following quick drill.

- "Read leather, yellow leather." Repeat these words slowly to begin, then speed up to the point where you are saying them as fast as you can.
- "Toy boat." This is another tongue twister that will help you to loosen the muscles of you lips and tongue.
- "Black slacks." I got this idea from Joe Bennett and the Sparkeltones' 1957 hit by the same name. When you say the word, keep you lips together and let them vibrate when you

say the letter "b". The word should sound like "B-B-B-B-Black slacks."

Everyday Conversation

Another excellent way to ensure that the concepts we discussed in this chapter become habit is to focus on them when you speak to people throughout your day. Thinking about improving your voice when you give presentations is not enough. Begin with the first person you greet in the morning and continue to practice with everyone you meet thereafter. Do this for 30 days and watch how your voice becomes more dynamic. Remember, after how you look, your voice is the key factor people will use in deciding if they like you, will listen to you, and will buy from you. Make it one of your greatest strengths.

THE FOOLPROOF STEPS
TO AVOID EMBARRASSMENT

See if this sounds familiar. You and your business partner are in your car en route to an important meeting with a prospective client. It's taken you months to set up this meeting. The outcome means thousands of dollars in future business for you. You turn to your partner and say, "Well, what should we cover?" She thinks for a few seconds and says, "Let's just wing it." Just winging it is certain to create disaster. It means no time went into customizing your message for your audience.

If you are like many people in sales, the steps I will suggest for you are not normally how you prepare. While they are foolproof, they won't be easy. That's because most successful sales professionals are entrepreneurial by nature. Your talents aren't in researching or following a system. Your strengths are in coming up with innovative ideas and presenting them to clients and prospects. I know, I'm the same way. Nonetheless, I proved the following to myself over and over:

Poor preparation = poor presentation
Good preparation = good presentation
Excellent preparation = excellent presentation

When former UCLA head football coach and current general manager of the San Francisco 49ers, Terry Donahue, was inducted into the College Football Hall of Fame in 2000, he prepared diligently for two weeks for a speech that lasted just over two minutes. Many of those in attendance felt that Terry's was one of the finest acceptance speeches they'd ever heard. His words provide wide counsel as you prepare for you next pitch: "A good process leads to a good result, whether it's a game or a speech. And when you've prepared, you have a sense of confidence that you don't have if you haven't."

Terry Donahue

In this chapter, you'll learn about a dynamic system that ensures you'll be well prepared for every presentation. The Power of the Pitch Process will take you through the steps you must take before and after your presentation. If you feel that you'll have difficulty following the process, enlist the assistance of someone on your team who likes working with systems.

STRATEGY SESSION

The first step in preparation is to conduct a strategy session to plan for the success of your presentation. The session may be just for you or a team if others are involved. Schedule the strategy session when you confirm the presentation date—at least 30 days prior to your presentation if possible. In many cases,

The Power of the Pitch Process

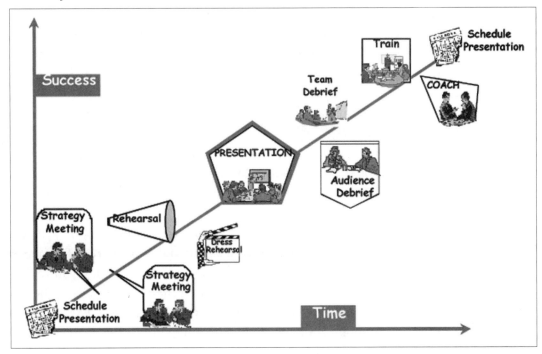

you may not have adequate advance notice, so do the best you can. At the strategy session, assess your knowledge in four areas.

Topic

Your audience will expect you to be an expert on the subject about which you will speak. Don't think you will win people over with the knowledge you gained from reading a few articles or books. Given the ease of obtaining information, people will demand in-depth knowledge.

This means that you must read a lot. You must become a *Holy Tearer*. Suppose you arrive early for a hair appointment. As you look around the reception area, what do you see on the tables and chairs? Magazines. Suppose you pick up a magazine and notice an interesting article that will enhance the knowledge you have of your topic. What do you do with the article? Cough loudly and rip the article out of the magazine. If that seems impolite, ask the receptionist to photocopy it for you. Let this concept of *Holy Tearer* be a metaphor for collecting information. Create a file folder for the articles you collect and label it RESEARCH. When the folder becomes too big, divide the articles into the most important topics in which you have an interest. Make similar files on your computer for the articles you download or scan. When you schedule your next presentation, you'll have files filled with ideas you can share with the audience.

Don't limit your reading to articles. Read every book you can find on the topic. Someone once opined that if you read five books on a subject you will become a subject matter expert. If you're like me, you may find it hard to find the time to read as many books as you would like. An excellent solution is to subscribe to some excellent book summary services. You'll get the essence of books in eight to ten pages. Some have companion audio recordings that you can use to transform your automobile into a mobile university. Please check the Resources section at the back of the book for a listing of some excellent book summary services.

Here's another great way to build your knowledge. Collect information about your everyday life experiences. Buy yourself a pocket-sized notebook with alphabetical tabs. Whenever something interesting happens to you, record it in your little book. One day, it might be something your child, grandchild, or significant other said or did, another day it might be a dreadful experience you had on your business trip, and another a superior way in which you handled a client issue. Increase the value of your little book by adding the jokes and quotes you hear. I started a little notebook about 15 years ago. Today it is one of my most valuable resources for preparing presentations.

Experts will also help you increase your knowledge of your topic. When you read an interesting article or book, dig deeper by interviewing the author. Authors are usually eager to discuss their topics with you. After all, they like the subjects so much that they spent hours researching and writing about them. I request interviews like these all the time and I've never had anyone turn me down.

Audience

Gaining knowledge about your audience is the only way to tailor your message to the audience's needs. Contact the person who scheduled your presentation and ask the following questions:

How many people will be in the audience? Two, five, a dozen, 100, 500? Each of these responses will tell you how to craft your presentation.

What are the demographics (ages, sexes, educational, income level)? If it's a small audience, obtain their resumes. Download this information from their Web sites or ask them to send it to you. Look for areas of commonality. Remember the Rock Star Attitude. People are persuaded by people they like. The probabilities are that they will like you if you attended the same school, like the same sports, or have had similar experiences.

Moreover, some prospects or clients will expect that you know about them. Take the case of Ron James. As the result of an introduction from a client, Ron scheduled a meeting with Theresa Spenser, the president of a large consulting firm.

Within the first two minutes of the meeting, Theresa interrupted Ron, "Let me ask you a question. How much do you know about our firm?"

"Well," said Ron, "you're a large firm based in Chicago and you have offices in many states."

"OK," continued Theresa. "I have another question for you. How much do you know about me?" Ron paused, small beads of perspiration forming on his forehead. "You're the president and you're in charge of the successful operation of the business," Ron said sheepishly.

"I'll tell you what, Ron," said Theresa as she stood up. "Why don't you come back when you've done your homework?"

Ron didn't know anything about the company or Theresa. Since the company was publicly traded, research would have been easy. He hadn't even bothered to read the president's resume, which was listed on the company's Web site.

What is the objective of the meeting? This is not your objective, but theirs. What are their expectations from meeting with you? Perhaps they want to know how you can help them. They may want you to merely listen to their concerns.

What are five issues that are faced by your group? People are motivated to act for two key reasons: pain or pleasure. Chances are they want to speak with you because they have a pain and they want you to remedy it. Dig deep into their pain. Find out what causes the key decision maker to wake up at 2:30 in the morning and not be able to go back to sleep. Don't tell them how you can help, just find out their issues.

What are the most significant events that have happened within your industry or group in the past year? This is a great question to help you understand what life has been like for the audience. You will find out if their business has been growing or shrinking, what management changes have taken place, and what new products and services are in the marketplace.

Is there any jargon or terminology I should use? Frequently, organizations will have their own words or phrases. By using their terminology, you will increase the likelihood of your identifying with the audience.

Are there any issues, events, or terms I should avoid? Sometimes this can make a big difference. If you were presenting to lawyers, accountants, and consultants, it would be *clients*, not *customers*. For private clubs and credit unions, it's *members*.

Who has spoken to you recently and how did they do? This is a great way to learn about competitors and your audience's expectations.

If I were to contact three people who were going to be at the presentation, who would they be? By interviewing additional people, you will further your knowledge of the audience.

Who are the experts in your industry or profession? This will allow you to do a search for articles or books by these individuals. Interview them to deepen your knowledge.

What industry magazines and newsletters do you read? Obtain copies of these to see the type of material your audience is being exposed to.

What are the best books about your industry or profession? Are there any books that are required reading at your organization? The knowledge you gain from books will help you customize your pitch. If *Good to Great* was one of the books that everyone at your prospect's firm read, mentioning at an appropriate time in your pitch the importance of "getting the right people on the bus" indicates that you share an interest in reading important business books.

What questions have I failed to ask? Sometimes people will have additional information they would like to share with you. This is often the point at which prospects discuss their innermost concerns.

After you've asked these questions, ask for their mission statement, organization chart, quarterly and annual reports, brochures, and business and marketing plans. By obtaining this information, you may know as much as the audience does. Please see the instructions for downloading The Power of the Pitch Questionnaire in the Resources section.

Competition

The third area to research as part of your strategy session is the competition. Who is offering products or services that compete with yours? List their strengths and weaknesses so that you will be able to differentiate yourself.

DETERMINE YOUR OBJECTIVES

It's vital that you be clear about your objectives, otherwise you won't achieve them. You will have one or both of the following objectives.

Persuade. Because we define a pitch as *anytime you speak with the intent to persuade,* this will certainly be the chief objective. Be sure you can answer the question: What do I want the audience to do? Perhaps it's to agree to buy your product or service at the end of your presentation. It may be to set up another meeting with others who are influential in the decision-making process. Or it might be to read your proposal and be ready to discuss it in a meeting the following week.

Inform. This may be a secondary objective. The question you must answer is: What do I want the audience to know? Keep in mind that the audience doesn't want to know everything you know about your product or service. Limit your message to three key points. We talk more about structure in Chapter 9.

CREATE AN OUTLINE

Do not write out your presentation. It's time-consuming and you may read or memorize it—not very exciting options for the audience. Instead, create an outline with a few words for each point. Use large font on a standard sheet of paper—one page for a five to ten minute presentation is sufficient. Beware of note cards. I observed a disaster scene one time when the speaker used note cards. Just as she started speaking, she gestured broadly, knocking the note cards off the table and scattering them on the floor. At that moment, her presentation was over; she never re-gained her composure after spending several minutes on the floor reorganizing the note cards.

REHEARSALS

The purpose of rehearsals is to be sure that you know your material. It may take you six times before you become comfort-able with the entire presentation. You want to get to the point where you glance at your notes occasionally for reference. This is an extemporaneous presentation, which means that you may change the way you say it every time you give it. It's not a written, memorized presentation, nor is it impromptu.

When you know your material, you'll feel confident. Remem-ber the 30-second Clock: the audience will perceive your confi-dence within the first 30 seconds of your presentation.

DRESS REHEARSALS

Make the last rehearsal a dress rehearsal. This is where you go through your presentation without stopping. Select a setting that replicates the one in which you will be making your pitch. Find a similar-sized room and set it up the way the room will be in which you will be presenting. If it's a conference room, speak from the appropriate end of the table. For a team presentation, place teammates in the proper locations. Solicit help from people not in the presentation to act as the audience and seat them in the proper locations. If you're using multimedia, set up the laptop computer and projector. The more realistic you can make it, the better.

Be sure to time your presentation. For team presentations, time the entire presentation as well as those of each team member. Time can be your biggest enemy. The real presentation typically lasts longer than the rehearsal. Even with no audience interaction, plan on your presentation being about 25 percent longer than it was in the rehearsal.

AUDIENCE DEBRIEF

After you give a presentation, ask the audience to give you comments on your presentation. Who better to give you valuable feedback than the people who just heard you? Conduct the debriefing in person or over the telephone as soon after your presentation as possible. The best time to schedule the debriefing is before you conduct the presentation.

If you're concerned about asking for feedback, don't be. I've never heard of a prospect to be unwilling to participate in a debrief, even when the prospect chose a competitor. A good way to position your debrief request is to say something like this: "We are continually looking to enhance the quality of our presentations. Would you be willing to answer a few questions for me about the presentation a few days after we meet?" Note that you're not asking for a justification of why the prospect did or didn't pick you. You're asking about the prospect's observations about the presentation.

Use the Power of the Pitch Audience Debrief Form to gather information. Please see the Resources section for instructions on how to download this form.

Go through all of the categories without asking questions about any one rating. If the prospect gave you a 2 in rapport and an 4 or 5 in all the other categories, ask the following type of question: "I notice you ranked me (us) a 2 in rapport. Just out of curiosity, tell me more about that." Suppose she said, "We didn't feel like you really connected with us. My partner said you never looked at him once." Although this is difficult to hear, don't be defensive. Instead thank her for her openness.

The information you have just learned is extremely valuable and will help you to win the business the next time you present. Most people don't conduct debriefings because they are uncomfortable with the idea. Not only does this give you a tremendous competitive advantage, the prospect will remember you. Who knows? Even if you don't gain their business they may reward you with the business if the person or company they chose doesn't perform.

TEAM DEBRIEF

Immediately following your presentation, e-mail the Power of the Pitch Team Debrief Form to each team member. Ask each team member to complete the form and return it to the team leader. Ask the team leader to compile the information and distribute it to each team member anonymously. For instructions on how to download this form, please see the Resources section.

If you gave the presentation by yourself, answer the questions as objectively as you can.

The Power of the Pitch Audience Debrief Form

Presentation Title: **Date:**

Individual Interviewed:

Title:

Organization:

1. What did you like best about the presentation?

2. How could the presentation be improved?

3. Were there any subjects not covered which you think should have been covered?

4. Any additional comments?

Rank the following elements of the presentation from 0 to 5

	Above Average		Average		Less Than Average	
	5	4	3	2	1	0
Rapport Developed						
Content Relevant to Your Needs						
Organization						
Subject Knowledge						
Delivery						
Effectiveness of Handout						
Audio/Visual Aids						
Proposal						
Overall Rating						

The Power of the Pitch Team Debrief Form

Title of Presentation:

Date:

Presenter	Strengths	Opportunities for Improvement

General comments on the presentation and how it can be improved in the future.

COACH

Once you've gotten this valuable information from the audience and your team, take action. For the person who received a "2" in the "Rapport we developed" category, coach him or her about the importance of eye contact. A good exercise is to video record that person giving a presentation and review the video, paying close attention to eye contact. Most people aren't aware of the lack of certain presentation skills. Your coaching will have a major impact on the person's future success as a presenter.

TRAIN

Enroll the individual who needs to enhance skills in a presentation skills program. If most people on the team could improve, enroll the entire team. Be sure the program you choose includes numerous video-coaching opportunities. Sitting in a seminar is not enough. To enhance your skills, you must give presentations and receive expert coaching. It's just like playing golf. You could go to dozens of lectures, but you won't start to become proficient until you swing a club, hit the ball, and have the pro tell you what you did wrong.

THE BENEFITS ARE ENORMOUS

We assisted Jones Lang LaSalle, a large international commercial real estate firm, in employing the Power of the Pitch Process. A major international bank made a strategic decision to outsource the management of its real estate. After reviewing proposals from a dozen firms, the bank invited five firms to make presentations. Bruce Ficke and his team at Jones Lang LaSalle were fortunate to be one of the five. If Bruce and his team were chosen, the bank would become the firm's largest account.

To prepare Bruce and his team to deliver the most important presentation of their careers, I coached the team through a series of strategy meetings, group and individual coaching sessions, rehearsals, and dress rehearsals. On the big day, Bruce and his team were confident, relaxed, and ready. Absent was the worry that grips most people before a big pitch. Thirty days later, Bruce received the call he had been waiting for. "Congratulations," said the bank officer, "we've decided to give the business to you."

When I debriefed the bank officer several months later, he said, "When the Jones Lang LaSalle team finished the presentation, I turned to one of my associates and said, 'That's the way to make a presentation.'"

I urge you to follow the steps in the Power of the Pitch Process. You'll enter the arena prepared and confident. Because this process takes discipline, most of your competition will not be as prepared. This will give you a tremendous advantage that will substantially increase your chances of winning the business.

8

THE PITCH, PART I
The Grabber

The executive management team carried on polite conversation as they waited for Bob Combs, a principal at an investment advisory firm, to propose how his firm would manage the company's pension plan. After ten minutes of idle chatter, the CFO Nancy Farmer, asked politely, "Bob, when are you going to begin your presentation?" To everyone's surprise, Bob replied, "I already have."

Bob committed a fatal error. He started a pitch and his audience didn't know it. Unimpressed by his nonchalant attitude, the team passed on Bob's proposal. This might not have been the case if Bob had begun his presentation with a strong introduction.

In this chapter you'll learn about the first of three parts of the pitch—a powerful way to introduce your pitch known as the Grabber. When used correctly, the Grabber will make your audience eager to listen to your pitch.

THE GRABBER

The purpose of the Grabber is twofold:

1. *Get your audience's attention.* As you begin your presentation, people in your audience may be thinking about their own personal issues. One may be thinking about the dry cleaning he needs to get on the way home, another about a new business strategy, and another about a dispute she just had with her assistant. The chances are high that they are not sitting there, primed and ready for the first words of wisdom to come out of your mouth. You must capture their attention.

2. *Focus the audience on your topic.* Many people think the purpose of the introduction is to warm the audience up. Frequently, you'll hear someone begin a presentation with a joke that doesn't have anything to do with the topic. After the joke, the speaker might say, "Oh, well anyway, let's get to what I'm going to speak about today." The joke does get the audience's attention, but because it's irrelevant, it does not focus people on the topic. You never want to hear yourself say, "Oh, well anyway."

FOUR COMMON MISTAKES

There are four common mistakes people make when they begin their presentations. Of course, these accomplish the opposite of the Grabber.

Apologizing

When you apologize, you only call attention to something about which the audience may not have been aware. Unfortunately, this happens in boardrooms around the world every day.

Recently, an advertising professional began his pitch to a prospective client by saying, "I'm sorry our president isn't able to kick the meeting off for you. He's asked me to step in for him."

Had it not been for the man's apology, the prospect wouldn't have known that the president had been planning to attend. Don't apologize for the temperature in the room, the size of the room, your lack of preparedness, or that the prospect or client has to be in this meeting listening to you on such a beautiful day.

Announcing the Topic

This flies in the face of common practice, since most people begin their presentations by stating their topic. Not only is announcing the topic trite, the people in your audience likely know why they are there.

Trivial Comments

Needless introductory comments may help warm up the presenter, but they bore the audience.

- "How's everybody doing today?" Do you really care? Is this a health discussion?
- "How about those Dodgers?" Is this a baseball presentation?
- "I sure am happy to be here in Chicago. This is such a great city—very cosmopolitan, yet very friendly." Unless the presentation involves travel, this also is irrelevant.

Referring to Notes

If there's one part of your presentation that you want to know cold, it's the introduction. When you look at your notes in the beginning of your presentation, it sends a signal to the audience that you don't know your material.

THE STAR SYSTEM

One of our clients once said to me, "The four common mistakes that you listed are usually how I begin my presentations. If I don't use any of them, what's left?" The answer is STARs, an acronym for four powerful ways to grab your audience's attention. Begin your presentation with one or two STARs. Remember, this is the introduction. Be sure the STAR you choose introduces your topic and not just one point in your presentation.

Let's suppose that you are a tax partner at an accounting firm. In preparing for a meeting with a prospect, you determined that the prospect was missing an opportunity to save $5 million a year because her company wasn't taking advantage of a certain tax strategy. Let's apply the STAR system to this scenario.

Startle

Start with a statement that will startle or shock the audience. You might begin by exclaiming, "Five million dollars! That's the size of your annual opportunity loss!" as you bring up a slide with "$5,000,000" in large numbers.

Tell a Story or a Joke

There are many types of stories, including case studies, examples, personal stories, fables, metaphors, and folk tales.

If you were to use a case study, you might discuss one of your clients who was in a position similar to that of your prospect and how your tax strategy provided the company with significant savings.

An appropriate well-told joke is another option. There are two sounds in life that we like the most. One is laughter. The other is your name, which we'll talk about later. When you can cause prospects to laugh, great things happen. They will feel better about themselves and, most importantly, about you. Think about it. When someone causes you to laugh, you have a good feeling about that person. When you feel good about her, you like her, and we have the Rock Star Attitude working at its best.

British Prime Minister Tony Blair uses humor frequently in his speeches. He did so extremely effectively in the introduction of his presentation to the Joint Meeting of the U.S. Congress on July 17, 2003. One of his unstated objectives was to convince Congress and the American people that efforts to combat terrorism and the war on Iraq were justified. Clearly this was a serious subject. Nonetheless, here's how he began his speech: "Mr. Speaker, Mr. Vice President, Honorable Members of Congress, I'm deeply touched by that warm and generous welcome. That's more than I deserve and more than I'm used to, quite frankly." With that the members of Congress broke into a roar of laughter as they stood to applaud. By poking fun at himself, he was able to humanize himself as he launched into a difficult presentation.

Unfortunately, humor is underused in most pitches. Why? Most people feel like they will embarrass themselves if they fail. If you feel this way, it's possibly due to a bad experience. Perhaps you attempted to use humor in a pitch and, despite your good intentions, no one laughed. That unfortunate experience may have caused you to say to yourself, "I can't tell jokes. I'll never use humor in my presentations again."

If you're hesitant to use humor in your pitch, start by taking small risks by using a funny word. After you've gotten a laugh, add another funny word to your next pitch. Soon you'll develop the confidence to add one-liners and, ultimately, jokes. Your objective is to have the audience laugh at least every five minutes. In Chapter 12, "Quick Say Something Funny!" I'll give you more suggestions on how to make that happen.

The pursuit of adding humor to your pitches may be one of your most fulfilling undertakings. You see, when you cause your audiences to laugh, your pitches will become more fun for the audience and, importantly, for you. Since making pitches is an important part of your life, why not make these experiences as pleasurable as possible?

Ask Questions

Ask two or three questions to be sure you have the audience's attention. Then, seek responses to your questions. It's important for you to develop rapport as early as possible. If you pose the question and answer it yourself, there won't be any interaction between you and the audience and, therefore, no opportunity to build a connection.

You might ask, "What is your guess as to the amount of money you're losing every year by not taking advantage of the tax laws? Is it $1 million, $3 million, or $5 million?"

Recite a Quote

The quote might be from the president's comments in the prospect's annual report, a testimonial letter you received from a client, or a well-known world figure.

As an example, you might begin with, "The British economist John Maynard Keynes said, 'The avoidance of taxes is the only pursuit that still carries any reward.' While I'm not here to talk with you about avoiding taxes, I do have a tax saving strategy that will pay you a big reward."

THE BENEFIT PREVIEW

Once you've gotten the attention of your client or prospect using one or more STARs, link the STAR to the body of your presentation with the Benefit Preview. There are three components of this linking tool.

Transition Statement

You will need a sentence or two to transition from the Grabber to the Benefit Preview.

"This savings could be yours simply by taking advantage of the tax laws."

The Preview

This is where you mention what you will discuss in the body of your presentation.

"During our discussion this morning, I'll guide you through a tax strategy that has produced excellent rewards for our clients."

In more formal presentations, such as those that are part of a Request for Proposal (RFP) process, prepare an agenda. Prior to the start of the meeting, place copies of the agenda at the places where you want the audience members to sit. Preview your presentation by reviewing the agenda.

The Benefit

The benefit answers the what's-in-it-for-them? (WIIFT) question. When you tell people about how they will benefit from your presentation, they will be much more likely to listen to you.

"I'm confident that as a result of our discussion, you'll see how the strategy will produce a $5 million tax benefit."

By combining the Grabber, Transition Statement, and Benefit Preview, we have created a powerful introduction.

"Five million dollars! That's the size of your annual opportunity loss. This savings could be yours simply by taking advantage of the tax laws. During our discussion this morning, I'll guide you through a tax strategy that has produced excellent rewards for our clients. I'm confident that as a result of our discussion, you'll see how the strategy will produce a $5 million tax benefit."

9

THE PITCH, PART II
The Persuasion Model

Ralph Jones, a partner in a real estate investment fund, recently made a pitch to five men and women charged with managing the investments of wealthy families. He began his presentation with a startling fact about the performance of shopping centers as an investment class. He continued by transitioning into the body of his presentation with a review of the key points he was going to make, coupled with the benefit the investors would receive by listening to his presentation. So far, he was following all the rules: he grabbed the audience's attention using a STAR and followed with a benefit preview.

But then his presentation went down hill quickly. He continued his pitch with a series of facts and figures, which he presented in an illogical manner. Moreover, it was difficult to tell where one point ended and the next began. As he droned on, one of the women got up and walked out of the room. Ten minutes later, one of the men left the meeting. Another man left a few minutes later. By the end of his fifty-minute presentation, all of the investment managers had left except one. When the managers talked later in the day, they unanimously concluded that his was the worst presentation they had ever heard. Despite Ralph's excellent introduction, he bored and confused his audience in the body of his presentation.

Because the body is the longest part of your pitch and where you develop the case for your products or services, it's critical that you organize it in a persuasive manner. If you don't, your listeners will become confused and bored. If they tune out, they will not buy. Forget about closing the sale, it won't happen. This chapter will show you how to structure the body of your presentation in a quick and easy manner that will lead a prospect to buy.

THE ISB MODEL

Structure your argument in a convincing manner by following the ISB Model.

- *I = Issue.* Begin by discussing your prospect's, client's, or team's issues, challenges, or objectives.
- *S = Solution.* Then provide your solution to their issues.
- *B = Benefit.* Complete the sequence by telling your client, prospect, or team how they will benefit from your solution.

I learned about the power of the ISB Model when I was a young stockbroker eager to become a top producer. I knew that the more prospects I saw, the greater were the chances I would achieve my production goals. As a result, I made hundreds of sales presentations. Retrospectively, many of them were awful.

One of those was a presentation I made to Jack Luden, a wealthy lawyer in Palm Desert, California. At the direction of my firm, I created a "flip book," which was three-ring binder containing information about the history, size, and services offered by my firm. In spite of the fact that it was July and 110°F, I wore my best salesman's uniform: navy blue suit, starched white shirt, and red tie. Jack, on the other hand, was dressed in a Hawaiian shirt, khakis, and loafers with no socks. If ever there was a violation of the One-Notch Principle, this was it. I was two or three notches above the way he dressed. By not being aware of how business people dressed in the desert, I had ensured that there would be no way Jack could identify with me. I'm sure his first impression of me was that of a city slicker who had come out to the hinterlands to take money from the unsuspecting commoners.

He invited me to sit in a large, comfortable chair in front of his large mahogany desk. We exchanged a few pleasantries, and then I pulled out my flipbook and placed it between us at the edge of his desk. I opened up the flipbook and began my pitch, first discussing my firm's proud history. Then I flipped to a map of our offices, pointing to each location. Next were some flattering articles about my firm. I was particularly proud of those.

As I turned to the next page, which listed the services we provided to investors, I heard a light snoring sound coming from Jack's direction. I looked up to see that Jack was asleep! In the middle of a sales presentation that I had so carefully crafted and rehearsed! How could he be so rude? Didn't he know I had driven two and one-half hours through snarling traffic from Los Angeles to Palm Desert and braved oven-like temperatures just to meet with him? I expected him to be grateful for the time and effort I had spent, to pay close attention to my presentation, to engage me in lively discussion, and to open a large stock portfolio with me. Instead, he was sound asleep and probably dreaming of basking in the cool breezes of Maui while sipping on a Mai Tai.

What I didn't realize at the time is that I was focusing my presentation on *me*. Not once did I mention *him*. Jack lost interest because I didn't focus on him. My entire presentation was about my firm and, although I was excited about our capabilities, I never once mentioned him. I doubt if he was interested in 10 percent of what I was talking about.

IT'S NOT ABOUT YOU

I failed to understand a basic rule of human nature—people are most interested in *themselves*. We are tuned to one mental radio station and that's station WIIFM—What's In It For Me. The message is: Don't talk about you, talk about me.

Unfortunately, some people don't understand the concept of WIIFM, as was the case with a pitch made by a team from a commercial real estate company to a committee from a large public company that was interested in outsourcing its real estate activities. The presentation team consisted of the president of the company, two senior brokers, and an analyst. The president began the pitch by giving the history of his company, and then moved to a map showing the firm's offices located in various cities around the country.

On the public company's five-person committee was a woman who headed the company's real estate department. As the president moved from the map of the firm's offices to his company's organization chart, the woman sighed and muttered something to the man next to her. The president then began to describe a transaction his firm had completed for a client. At this point, the woman sighed loudly and shook her head. Unfazed, the president launched into a review of a second successful transaction.

"Oh, my God!" exclaimed the woman in a voice loud enough that everyone in the room could hear. Seemingly oblivious to the woman's growing impatience, the president presented a third example.

As the president put up a slide showing a photograph of a fourth building that was part of another successful transaction, the woman slammed her hand down on the table and said, "Will you stop talking about your company and tell us what you can do for us!"

Guess what the president said? He said, "I will in just a minute. But, first, I have one more transaction that I'd like to discuss with you." The president spoke for fifteen minutes about his company. Not once did he mention the prospect. In case there is any doubt in your mind, the real estate company did not get the business.

Imagine that you trip down some steps and break your arm. Immediately, a friend takes you to the emergency room of the closest hospital. After you fill out the required information, a nurse escorts you to a doctor's office.

Sitting behind his desk is a man named Dr. About Me. Dr. Me rises, walks over to you, shakes your hand, and says, "Hello. It's a pleasure to meet you. Since we've never met, I thought I'd take a few minutes to tell you about my practice. I graduated from the University of Virginia with a B.A. biology." Dr. Me proudly points to a certificate hanging on the wall and continues, "I graduated from Georgetown University Medical School, did my residency at the University of North Carolina Medical Center in Chapel Hill, and then came to this hospital. That was 19 years ago. My practice has grown tremendously since then, and my medical group now has offices in four hospitals as you can see on the map to your right."

Meanwhile, your arm is throbbing with excruciating pain! You become angry and resentful. How could Dr. Me be so self-absorbed that he is oblivious to your pain? Can't he see the grimace on your face, the perspiration on your forehead, the clinched teeth?

Of course this would never happen. The first question the doctor would ask you is, "What happened to *you?*" Not "What happened to *me?*" Then he would inspect your arm carefully, pressing and pulling on it in an effort to determine the extent of your injury. Next he would take an X ray of your arm so he could be sure of his initial assessment.

Unknowingly, I had treated Jack Luden in the same way Dr. Me would have. My presentation was all about me. After all, human nature favors a focus on oneself. As soon as a little girl learns to speak, she says "my dolly" and rips the toy out of the hands of a devastated playmate. A teenager nonchalantly moves in front of skiers as he patiently inches his way forward in a chairlift line. A woman in a Honda cuts other drivers off on the freeway. The focus is on WIIFM. As a presenter, you must forget about yourself and focus on WIIFT, or what's in it for *them?* The woman you're interviewing with doesn't care about your travels throughout Asia; she's interested in how you will help her become more successful if she hires you. The selection committee isn't interested in the history of your organization; they want to know how you can help them achieve their goals. By answering the WIIFT question, you will address what motivates your client, prospect, or team.

Remember the pain or pleasure motivators. As a professional attempting to convince someone to buy your product or service, you are in the business of relieving pain. Never once did I tell the lawyer how I could relieve his pain. I didn't even ask him what his pain was.

I *assumed* that he wanted to know everything about my company. I *assumed* that he would listen intently and with great interest to everything I said as I turned from one page of my flipbook to the next. After I had finished my presentation, I *assumed* he would select from several of the services my firm provided and I would close the sale. I didn't realize that he had a very specific pain and only was interested in how he could relieve it. The first rule of persuasion is simply this: if you want to persuade someone, you must find out what his or her pain is and then focus on it first and now.

BEGIN WITH THEIR ISSUES

As I mentioned, the *I* in the ISB Model stands for issues. This is the pain. What are the key issues, challenges, objectives, or concerns that are causing the CEO to lose sleep? As we discussed in Chapter 7, this is information you would have uncovered in preparing for the pitch.

State the three most important issues an individual or organization has and then ask for confirmation or additions. The prospect may give you new information, which will help you in further addressing needs.

Pain frequently is centered in one or more of the following:

- *Time:* Achieving a goal on time
- *Money:* Making and/or protecting it, accomplishing a task at or under budget
- *Success:* Achieving success or greater success
- *People:* Too many, not enough and/or lack of competencies
- *Space:* Too much, not enough and/or the wrong kind
- *Quality:* Not high enough, maintaining it

In discussing pain with an individual, it's important that you dig deep into the pain. Make the prospect suffer mentally. Get her emotionally involved. Let him feel the pain. Ask the following questions:

- What will happen if you don't resolve the issues that you have?
- How much time, money, or opportunity will you lose?
- Who else will be impacted by the lost time, money, or opportunity?

Recently, I scheduled an appointment with Donna Morris, who was in charge of one of the business units of a large consulting firm. Donna told me over the phone that she was not happy with her group's performance results and that they were losing too much business to the competition. When we sat down to meet, I began by confirming her key issues and followed with some questions to fully uncover the pain.

"Donna," I asked, "what would you say is the average fee you charge a client?"

"On average, $400,000," she responded.

I continued, "Approximately how many new business pitches does your team make a month?"

"About ten," she replied.

"And what is the closing ratio of the pitches you give?" I asked.

"Over the last year, it's been about 10 percent," she said disappointedly.

This led to my next question, "What would you like your closing ratio to be?"

"Our business plan calls for it to be 20 percent," she said.

"Let me see, Donna," I said. "If you're making ten presentations a month and closing 10 percent, that's one a month. Since your average fee is $400,000, your monthly fee from new business is $400,000 or $4.8 million a year. Correct?"

"Yes, that's right," replied Donna.

"So, by not achieving your projected closing ratio of 20 percent, you are generating nearly $5 million less in revenue than projected," I concluded.

"Yes," said Donna uncomfortably, "that's correct."

"Donna," I continued, "who is impacted by this shortfall in revenue?"

"Well, my team," she said.

"And how are they impacted?" I asked.

"Since we are on a bonus system, our bonuses were down significantly last year and will be again this year. As a result, morale is at an all-time low. Recently, we've lost some of our top people," concluded Donna.

"What is the impact on you?" I asked.

"If my team doesn't achieve its revenue projections, I will probably lose my job," confessed a dejected Donna.

By this time in our conversation, Donna is suffering. But, remember, the idea is to delve deep into the pain and uncover the important issues. This is not a pleasant experience for people—most would like to avoid the subject. Nonetheless, you must be vigilant. You must stay with it. When you see the doctor, he or she may make you feel worse before she makes you feel better. When she presses and pulls your broken arm, you might even scream in agony.

I continued with my line of questioning, "Who else is impacted by your revenue shortfall?"

"The shareholders," replied Donna.

"How will they be impacted?" I asked.

"Since my group is a catalyst for generating business in the other business lines of the company, earnings will decline and the stock price will drop," Donna responded.

You may be thinking that I had probed enough into Donna's pain. However, you could continue as long as the individual is willing to have this conversation with you.

I concluded with one last question, "Donna, I can see that every member of your team is impacted, you are impacted, and the shareholders are impacted. Is anyone else affected by the inability of your group to achieve its goals?"

Donna thought for a minute, and then said, "Every one of us on the management team has stock and stock options. Their net worths would be impacted."

By asking Donna a few questions, I helped her identify the key issues:

- Her group is producing $5 million less revenue than projected.
- Her team's morale is low.
- Shareholders, management, and Donna are negatively impacted.

Keep in mind that the objective in discussing the issues is to focus on the person's or company's pain. Do not mention anything about you or your firm or how you might be able to help until you move on to the next stage.

PRESENT YOUR SOLUTION

Having discovered or confirmed the issues, you then move to the *S* in ISB, the solution. This is where you discuss your solution to the individual's or organization's issues. Here you discuss how you will help them. This is not where you list all the services you provide, but those that specifically meet the needs of the prospect.

In the case of Donna, I described our solution by leading her through the following diagram of our process, which includes

The Great Communicator Program

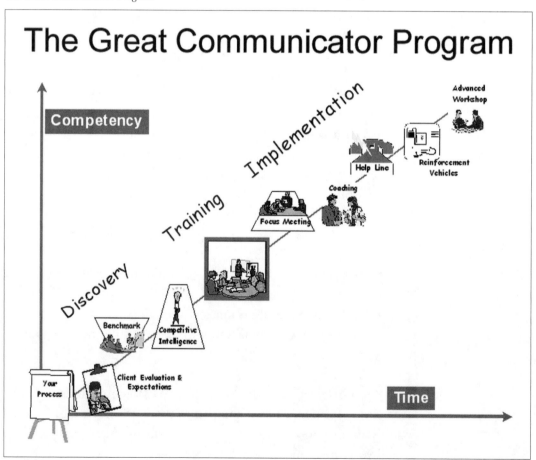

numerous products and services that will help her team win more business.

We gave our solution a name and trademarked it. I got this idea of creating a comprehensive program and giving it a name from Dan Sullivan, President of The Strategic Coach Inc.® in Toronto, Canada.

I encourage you to create a trademarked name for the solution you provide clients. Here are some examples:

- The Strategic Coach Program™
- The Wealth Maximizer Process™
- The Estate Value Protection Solution™
- The Author Success Program™
- The New Car Satisfaction System™
- Your solution: The _____

Naming your solution gives it much more validity. Next, list each step and give it a name. By naming each step, you increase the perceived value of your process. You may have up to a dozen different components. The steps to The Great Communicator Program are as follows:

- Rainmaker Analysis
- 360° Feedback
- The Benchmark
- Competitive Intelligence Analyzer
- The Communication Power Workshop
- Monthly Focus Meetings
- The Help Line
- The Coaching Session
- The Great Communicator Program Review Series
- The Advanced Workshop

The steps in your solution:

- _____
- _____
- _____
- _____
- _____
- _____
- _____
- _____
- _____
- _____
- _____
- _____

Once you have taken prospects and clients through your process, they will understand how you can help them. Now it's time for the final component in the body of your presentation.

PEOPLE BUY BENEFITS, NOT FEATURES

The *B* in the ISB Model stands for the benefits the individual or organization will receive by using your solution. Emphasizing the benefits is important because of the key sales premise: people buy benefits, not features.

Several years ago, I went into an automobile dealer's showroom to buy a Porsche. There in the middle of the showroom was this beautiful red Targa with the top off. The shiny exterior glistened under the lights. I could smell the scent of the tan leather. As I walked around the car admiring its curvaceous, sleek lines, an automobile salesman walked up to me and asked, "Are you interested in buying a Porsche today?"

"Yes," I replied.

"Tell me," continued the salesman, "why do you want to buy a Porsche?"

"Because they're fast," I said with a childish grin.

"Oh, yes. Porches are fast," confirmed the salesman. "Do you like roller coasters?"

"Yes, I do," I responded.

"You know that first steep incline that you go up?" the salesman asked as he extended his right arm to better describe the roller coaster's steep angle of ascent.

"Yes," I said as I looked in the direction he'd indicated.

"You know that feeling of excitement as you move slowly up to the highest point in the amusement park?" he asked.

"Yes," I answered as I felt the familiar tingle in my body.

"You rest there momentarily," he continued, "and then plunge down a 150-foot vertical drop in four seconds, reaching a speed of 70 miles an hour and causing your hair to stand on end and your heart to jump out of your body. Do you know that feeling?"

"Oh, yes, I do!" I exclaimed as I relived my last great roller coaster experience.

"Well, that's exactly the way you're going to feel when you take this Porsche from second to third gear," proclaimed the salesman.

"I'll take it!" I shouted.

The automobile salesman sold me on the benefits of owing a Porsche. He talked about how I would feel behind the wheel of this machine. Never once did he mention a feature. He could have said, "Oh, yes, Porches are fast. That's primarily because of the way they're engineered. They all have aluminum, six cylinder, overhead cam, rear-mounted engines." As many people do, he could have continued with more features and ultimately lost the sale. People buy benefits, not features.

Sometimes people have difficulty differentiating between a feature and a benefit. A feature describes a product or service; a benefit describes what the feature will do for you. For example, the steps you take in your quality control process are features. The fact that your process will eliminate errors is a benefit.

Provide the audience with three benefits, and link the benefits back to the issues. In my presentation to Donna, the benefits were as follows:

- Her group will meet their revenue projection.
- There will be renewed team camaraderie and spirit.
- Shareholders and management will be pleased with Donna and her team.

Now that we've discussed how to use the ISB Model, let's spend a minute on sequence. Of course, you could discuss all the issues, your entire solution, and all of the benefits. This would be appropriate if the solution addressed the client's or prospect's issues, as was the case when I presented my solution to Donna Morris. In this case, you would use The Power of the Pitch Outline. For instructions on how to download this form, please see the Resources section.

Alternatively, you could cover the first issue, the corresponding solution, and the related benefit, and then repeat the sequence for the second and third issues. This sequencing works well in team presentations where each team member has a solution that is linked to an issue. In this case, use The Power of the Pitch Outline for Teams. See the Resources section for instructions on downloading this form.

The ISB Model is a powerful method of structuring your persuasive argument. Since ISB works in business *and* personal venues, you'll have daily opportunities to use it with your spouse, children, grandchildren, and friends.

The Power of the Pitch Outline

Title: Date:

Audience:

Objectives:

Introduction

Intro (STAR):

Benefit Preview (Agenda + WIIFT):

Body

Intro (STAR):

Benefit Preview:

Issue:

Edutain:

Solution:

Edutain:

Benefit:

Edutain:

Q & A

Conclusion

Conclusion (STARUS):

The Power of the Pitch Outline for Teams

Title: **Date:**

Audience:

Objectives:

Introduction

Intro (STAR):

Benefit Preview (Agenda + WIIFT):

Body

Issue 1

Intro (STAR):

Benefit Preview:

Issue:

Edutain:

Solution:

Edutain:

Benefit:

Edutain:

Conclusion (STARUS):

Issue 2

Intro (STAR):

Benefit Preview:

Issue:

Edutain:

Solution:

Edutain:

Benefit:

Edutain:

Conclusion (STARUS):

Issue 3

Intro (STAR):

Benefit Preview:

Issue:

Edutain:

Solution:

Edutain:

Benefit:

Edutain:

Conclusion (STARUS):

Q & A

Conclusion

Conclusion (STARUS):

THE RULE OF THREE

People don't want to know everything you know. More than anyone in modern history, Abraham Lincoln understood this value of brevity. At 272 words, his Gettysburg Address took less than three minutes to deliver. Former Secretary of State, Edward Everett, a highly talented orator and the keynote speaker at Gettysburg, spoke for two hours. Although Everett's speech was regarded as an excellent recounting of the recent events, it is Lincoln who is remembered for his brilliance.

The Rule of Three states that people will remember three key points, not ten or twelve. When you organize your presentation using the ISB Model, identify the three most important issues, components of your solution, and benefits. In addition, use the principle as a powerful tool to organize your responses to questions and for presentations where your objective is to inform.

For example, the selection committee of a country club was charged with interviewing candidates for the general manager's job. The objective of each of the four male candidates was to convince the committee members why he was the best man for the job. The committee asked each of the applicants to describe his leadership style. All of the men responded with long, drawn-out answers that covered ten to fifteen leadership characteristics, some even repeated each other. Larry Moss was the exception.

"There are three characteristics of my leadership style," responded Larry. "The first is team-building. I build teams where everyone contributes his or her own unique talents to the team." He then told the committee how he had built a successful team in his current position.

"The second characteristic that describes my leadership style is accountability," Larry continued. He described this concept further and gave an example.

"The third characteristic of my leadership style is innovation," said Larry. Then he described some of the innovations he brought to his current employer.

"Those are the characteristics of my leadership style: team building, accountability, and innovation," Larry summarized.

Larry nailed this question in less than four minutes. There was no rambling or repeating. He gave the committee three characteristics, coupled with appropriate examples, and he was done. It was clear to the committee that, because of the way he handled just this one question, he was their man.

Regardless of the type and length of your presentation, from a media interview to a speech at a shareholders meeting, get in the habit of using the Rule of Three regularly and you'll be thrilled with the results.

USE SMOOTH TRANSITIONS

As you move from one point to the next, be sure to let the audience know where you are going by using smooth transitions. Avoid merely stating the next point as if you were reading from an outline. For shorter points, use words or phrases such as:

- As importantly . . .
- The second element is . . .
- Let's take a look at another reason . . .

For longer points, summarize the point before moving onto the next. Sometimes people can become lost in the middle of a presentation. By summarizing periodically, you'll help people to stay in your presentation rather than giving up and drifting off because they are lost.

THE MAGIC OF EDUTAINMENT

Adults learn best when they are entertained. The people listening to you will think about something other than what you are saying about every five minutes. If you don't keep them entertained, they're going to change the channel and start thinking about something else. You might be on the sales channel, but their internal remote controls have flipped over to the vacation channel.

Edutain with STARs

There are two ways to keep the prospects edutained. The first is to use STARs to illustrate your key points. Remembering the ISB Model, you would first discuss an issue and then perhaps choose the *A* for ask questions. When your present the solution, you might edutain by *T*, telling a story about how your product or service resolved an issue similar to the one your prospect is experiencing.

Edutain with Audiovisuals

The second way to edutain is to use visual aids. When employed effectively, visuals will more than double retention. We retain about 20 percent of what we see *or* hear. But, we retain 50 percent of what we see *and* hear.

When you speak with people and show them an impactful graph to develop a point, you will help them remember your message. Please note the adjective *impactful*. Text slides that merely mimic what you are saying may do more harm than good. We'll

20–50 Retention

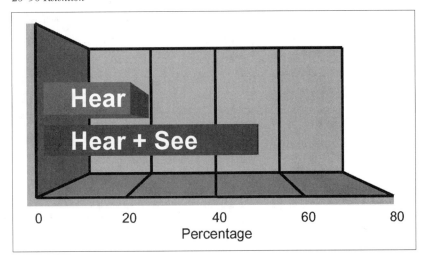

talk about visuals in Chapter 14, but for now, know that they can be very valuable when used appropriately.

THE PRINCIPLE OF PERSONALIZATION

Have you ever spoken to prospects or clients and about halfway through your pitch you noticed that they seemed disinterested? If you looked very carefully, you might have seen two words on their foreheads: "Who cares?"

When you see the who-cares? expression, it means you are not personalizing your message for them. Remember, the prospect is interested in WIIFM.

In order to connect with your audience, minimize the use of the pronoun *I* and maximize the use of the pronouns *you* and *we*. Perhaps you've heard sales professionals go on about how *I* did this and how *I* did that. Oh, how great *I* am. *I* excludes the members of your audience; *you* and *we* includes them.

In Chapter 8, I pointed out that one of the two sounds that we most like is laughter. The other is the sound of our name. The Principle of Personalization states that not only should you use the personal pronouns *you* and *we,* you should use people's names. Occasionally using people's names builds rapport and makes people feel like they are an integral part of your presentation.

Similarly, when making a pitch to several people, avoid using words that depersonalize your message, such as the following:

- All of you
- Everyone in the room
- Each and every one of you
- You people
- Everybody
- You guys

For example, instead of saying, "What this means for everyone in the room," say, "What this means for you."

Moreover, rather than using the name of a company, use the personal pronoun *you.* Instead of saying, "Here's what we will do for ABC Company," say, "Here's what we will do for you." Since the word *you* is both singular and plural, people in the audience will think you are speaking directly to them.

By using the Principle of Personalization, you will connect with each person in your audience. Couple this principle with two to four seconds of eye contact per person and you will develop strong rapport, which will significantly increase the likelihood that your pitch will be successful.

YOUR UNIQUE SELLING PROPOSITION

Advertisers use this expression in determining what causes you to choose one product over the other when you walk down the grocery store aisle. Prospects will be persuaded to buy your product or service if it provides them a value they cannot readily obtain. The concept is based on the premise that people buy difference, not similarity.

When my daughter, Gabi, was about six years old, we went grocery shopping one day. One of the products on our shopping list was cereal. Gabi was especially fond of Frosted Cheerios. As we passed by the cereal section, I noticed that a box of the generic version of the cereal, Frosted Toasted Oats, was $1.87, compared to $3.68 for Frosted Cheerios. Since the Frosted Toasted Oats was half the price, I quickly placed the box in our shopping cart.

In an instant, Gabi reached in the shopping cart, grabbed the cereal box, and demanded, "What is this?"

"Frosted Cheerios," I replied.

"Dad, this is not Frosted Cheerios," she said as she summarily dismissed the box of Frosted Toasted Oats. "This is Frosted Cheerios!" and she held up a box of the real thing.

I reached over and picked up the box of Frosted Toasted Oats. "Yes, these are Frosted Cheerios, Gabi. Look. See the little toasted oats with the sugar on them?" I asked, pointing to the photo on the front of the box. Wanting no more of this foolish conversation, Gabi pushed the shopping cart ahead as I stood there holding the box of Frosted Toasted Oats. Even though the box of Frosted Cheerios was nearly twice the price as Frosted Toasted Oats, I decided to relent. Maybe Gabi had a point and, although I was footing the tab, she was the end user, the consumer, and I wanted her to eat the darn things.

What Gabi demonstrated is the power of a unique selling proposition. Indeed, General Mills spent millions of dollars convincing Gabi its product was superior. When people perceive your product or service to be uniquely different from anything else they can buy in the marketplace, price is not an issue. Look for uniqueness in the following areas:

- Product
- Process
- Service
- Experience
- Knowledge

Take a few minutes and write down six uniquenesses you offer.

1. _____
2. _____
3. _____
4. _____
5. _____
6. _____

Of the six uniquenesses you listed, can any other firm or individual make the same claims? If so, look for ways to enhance your service or product so that it truly is unique.

When you make your pitch, emphasize your uniquenesses. If you are speaking with a prospect who does business internationally, discuss the fifty-two offices you have around the world.

Focusing on your unique selling proposition will keep you out of a price war. When there is no difference between one product or service and another, you are in the commodity business—you are competing based on price, and if you don't have the lowest price, you lose. If you don't want to compete for business like this, develop products or services that differentiate you from the competition. Then highlight them in your pitch.

GHOSTING

You will want to use this powerful tool in every presentation. In ghosting, you point out the weakness of competitors without specifically mentioning them. Suppose you are a construction management company interviewing with the management team of a hospital who is going to build a new facility. Let's further suppose that you have extensive experience in building hospitals and that the competitors have little or none.

Clearly, one of your uniquenesses is your hospital experience. The way you ghost the competition is by pointing out how critical it is that the hospital team selects a firm with significant hospital experience. Add proof to this statement by relating a disaster story about a hospital that was built by a construction manager with little hospital experience.

THE ELEVATOR PITCH

When a speaker was told that he only had ten minutes to give his thirty-minute speech, he stepped up to the microphone and announced to the audience, "I was just informed that I only have ten minutes to make my ten points." At the back of the room a man yelled, "Start on point number nine."

Every pitch you make about the solution you provide clients must have a shorter version. When you arrive for a meeting, if the prospect tells you that you only have fifteen minutes instead of thirty, you'd better be ready—and the answer for being allocated less time is not to talk faster.

Be prepared to adjust the amount of information you are going to tell people with the time you are given. Typically, the shorter the time, the more difficult it is to make your pitch. The Elevator Pitch falls into this category. This is the pitch that you must give within the time it takes an elevator to go an average of twenty-five floors. The key point is not necessarily that you are in an elevator, it's that you only have a few seconds to persuade a prospect to take action.

Whenever you find yourself in an elevator, cocktail reception, or any space where you have a captive, albeit temporary, audience, use it as an opportunity to prospect. Start with the question, "What do you do?" Then listen carefully and ask polite questions. If the prospect meets your qualifications, make a short pitch when the prospect concludes the answer. Most likely the person will ask in return, "What do you do?" Do not, under any circumstances, answer with your profession, for example, "I'm a life insurance agent, lawyer, stockbroker, real estate broker, accountant, banker, investment advisor, salesman, etc."

Such a response is sure to stop all conversation. The person to whom you're speaking is likely to say, "That's nice," and seek a rapid retreat. Instead, use a benefit statement, such as, "I help people retire with more money than they ever thought possible, pay as little in taxes as possible, purchase the assets they always dreamed about, protect their wealth, etc."

You want the prospect to ask the important follow-up question: "Really, how do you do that?" So you can say, "Unfortunately, we don't have enough time for me to explain it to you right now, but if you'll give me your card, I'll be happy to give you a call." That's it. That's your Elevator Pitch. Once you have the prospect's card, call to set up an appointment. Then you'll have the time to lead this individual through ISB and close the business.

By employing the methods we discussed for the body of your pitch, you can be sure that your closing ratio will go up dramatically. As a recap, please remember to:

- Structure your persuasive pitch with the ISB Model.
- Eliminate verbosity with the Rule of Three.

- Keep the prospect interested with the magic of edutainment.
- Develop rapport with the Principle of Personalization.
- Differentiate yourself with the your unique selling proposition.
- Eliminate the competition by ghosting.
- Practice your Elevator Pitch.

10

THE PITCH, PART III
The Power Close

Once you've discussed the customer or prospect's issues, your solution, and the benefits of using your solution, it's time to conclude your pitch. This is where you ask for the order. For some, this is an extremely difficult task. Perhaps it is for you, too. Think of it this way, if you don't ask, prospects won't make a decision. Let's face it, most people are procrastinators. If you leave it up to them to "think about it and let you know," you could be waiting a long time. Meanwhile, a competitor with better persuasion skills will close them. Let's take a look at a method that will ensure that your prospects and clients take action.

THE Q&A

Before you conclude your pitch, take a few minutes for any questions the audience may not have previously asked. Note that the Q&A comes *before* the conclusion. Most presenters make the mistake of saving it for the final part of their presentations. Ask for questions before the conclusion for one chief reason. Suppose someone asks you a difficult question and your response is less than stellar. This now becomes the audience's last, and perhaps lasting, impression of you.

Because most people are accustomed to presenters saving the Q&A period for last, you must alert audiences that you will follow with a conclusion. A statement like the following will serve the purpose: "Before I conclude my presentation, I'll take a few minutes for any additional questions you may have. Who has the first question?" Note the question, "Who has the first question?" In a pitch, you want the audience to ask questions before you conclude. These questions may be the objections, which, if unanswered, might prevent the audience from doing what you want it to do. By using the word *first,* you encourage the audience to ask questions. Once you've answered the questions, it's time to conclude.

PURPOSE OF THE CLOSE

The purpose of the close is to close the deal. There is no new information in the conclusion. Conclude by using one or a combination of STARUS. This method adds two new ways to the STARs that you use in the introduction and throughout your presentation.

THE STARUS SYSTEM

Startle

If you used a startling statement in the Grabber, you might repeat it to further emphasize the point. However, given that your objective is to persuade the audience, you will need to combine the *S* (startle) with either an *A* (ask questions) or a *U* (urge).

Tell a Story or a Joke

As with a startling statement, telling a story or a joke will not be sufficient. You will need to add either an *A* or a *U*.

Ask Questions

This is where you ask for the order. If the client or prospect can make a decision on the spot, this is your best method. Start with a broad question that measures the audience's interest, as follows:

> You: "How does this (product or service) sound?"
> Prospect: "It sounds great."
> You: "Terrific, can we get started today?"

As you know, most of the time it's not that easy. Be prepared with some follow-up questions:

> You: "How does this (product or service) sound?"
> Prospect: "I'm not sure."
> You: "Say more about that."

The prospect will now give you one or more objections, which you must be prepared to answer. When you do, you've closed the business. In Chapter 13, you'll learn about a powerful method for overcoming any objection your prospect or client will have.

Recite a Quote

Again, the quote will not be sufficient. You will need to combine this with either an *A* or a *U*.

Urge. With an urge, you encourage the audience to do what you want it to do. Use the urge when the audience cannot make a decision at that time. Perhaps the individual or committee must hear other proposals. In this case, the urge might sound something like this, "I urge you to give us the opportunity to work with you. Together, we will create a brand that will dominate the marketplace."

Summarize. A summary provides a neat way of wrapping up your pitch. However, you still need a call to action. Add either an *A* or a *U* and you have a winning combination.

THE MEANINGLESS CLOSE

There are two words that you do not want to use to close your pitch: *Thank you.* The words *thank you* are nothing more than an anticlimactic end to an otherwise strong conclusion.

Just image Patrick Henry concluding his famous speech like this: "And as for me, give me liberty or give me death! Thank you."

Ending with *Thank you* isn't a way of showing appreciating for the audience's attention; it's a substitute for *The End.* In older movies the words *The End* would appear after the last scene. But, sensing that audiences have gotten more sophisticated, film editors have stopped providing us with a statement of the obvious.

Not saying *Thank you* means that you must know your conclusion very well. There can be no question on the part of your audience that you have completed your presentation. For that reason, it's imperative that you rehearse the conclusion to the point that you have it memorized. Then, when it's time to conclude, let the power of your conclusion signal to the audience that you are finished.

11

TELL ME A STORY, PLEASE!

My father was a great storyteller. Every night before I went to bed, I asked him to tell my brother and me a story. His stories were usually scary—they often featured a huge black bear in the woods that surprised and chased (but never hurt) unsuspecting campers and hikers. Perhaps some of my dad's storytelling ability rubbed off on me, because my sixth grade teacher frequently called on me to tell the class one of those scary stories I'd come to love. For 30 minutes at a time, a group of 30 12-year-olds sat in silence as I regaled them with tales of the big black bear and the campers who barely escaped its wrath.

Why did we, as children, beg for someone to tell us a story? Better yet, why do we, as adults, flock to movie theaters, buy and rent DVDs by the dozens, and read more books than in any point in history? We love to be entertained. We want people to tell us stories.

Given our thirst for storytelling, it's imperative that you pepper your pitches with stories. It's the primary reason we included stories in the STAR System (T=Tell a Story). In this chapter, you'll learn to become a master storyteller.

THE PURPOSE OF STORIES

Entertain

The average person watches 3.5 hours of television a day—the majority of which is for entertainment purposes. Those same people are sitting in your audience, and they want you to entertain them. If you don't, they will "tune you out."

Create Greater Memory Value

Your team members, clients, and prospects will remember the stories you tell them long after the facts and figures you give them. Just think back to a story a teacher told you in high school or college. If you're like me, you won't remember the various points the teacher made, but you will remember the story.

GUIDELINES

The Story Must Be Relevant

This is the first rule of using stories in your pitches. If your story doesn't directly relate to the point you're making, don't use it.

I remember a story a minister told in church one Sunday when I was about 14. The story was about a wealthy man who commissioned a homebuilder to build him the finest home money could buy. The man gave the builder a check for the cost of the home and asked him to let him know when it was finished. The builder decided that this was an opportunity for him to make an extra profit by substituting inferior building products. When the home was finished, the new owner was so pleased with the results that he informed the builder that he was giving the home to him as a gift. It was a great story about the importance of being honest.

Live the Story

Paint vivid word pictures that make your story come alive. In the story about the wealthy man and his new home, the chaplain described the inferior products the builder used:

When the builder set out to frame the house, he purchased lumber that had been exposed to the elements and attacked by termites. He figured the owner would never know the truth. Instead of the rich mahogany paneling, which the builder had promised for the expansive library, he used plywood treated with a mahogany stain. He substituted a manufactured marble veneer for the floor in entryway that was supposed to be of fine Italian marble. Throughout the house, the builder cut corners and substituted inferior materials in his effort to make an extra profit.

Recreate the dialogue

Use dialogue to recreate conversations. Don't merely refer to a conversation as in the following:

After a year of construction, the house was completed. When the builder showed the wealthy man his new home he was pleased. So pleased was the man that he told the builder he was going to give him a gift. He was going to give him the house.

In this telling of the story there is no dialogue. There is merely reference to the conversation. Recreate the dialogue as in the following:

> After a year of construction, the house was completed. When the builder showed the wealthy man his new home, the wealthy man said, "You have truly lived up to your reputation. This house is beautiful! I can see by the quality of the materials that you have done exactly as I wished."
>
> "Thank you, sir," replied the builder. "As you requested, I have spared no expense."
>
> "I am so pleased with this house," said the wealthy man, "that today I'm going to give you a gift. Today I give you this house."

Avoid the Extraneous

Have you ever heard people tell stories that go on and on? You can get so lost in the minutiae of the story that you tune out. Rehearse your stories to rid them of unnecessary information. If they seem long to you, you can be sure they will seem long to the listeners.

Long Story, Big Ending

If you have a long story, it better have a powerful conclusion. If it doesn't, your audience will feel like you wasted their time.

Don't Always Make Yourself the Hero

Look for opportunities to tell stories about yourself where you've made mistakes. After all, you're only human, and your audience will appreciate your acknowledgement of that fact. Avoid the temptation to continually puff yourself up by telling people how well you handled various issues.

Look to reduce the number of *I* stories by using a third party to replace yourself where you are the hero of the story. Instead, use a fictitious third person as the central character of your story, as in the following:

> One of our clients, Fred Jones, the 56-year-old president of an advertising agency, had to make a pitch to an internet search firm comprised of men and women in their twenties.

Another strategy is to substitute the audience wherever possible by using the pronoun *you,* as in the following:

> Imagine that you are in your mid-fifties and the president of an advertising agency. One day, you get a request to make a pitch to an Internet search firm comprised of men and women in their twenties.

Practice on Everyone

You never want to hear yourself telling a story to an audience for the first time. Your timing may be off, you may include extraneous information, or you may forget part of the story. Avoid these mistakes by practicing your stories several times before you include them in your pitches. An excellent way to work on stories is by appropriately interjecting them in conversations with friends and associates. Don't set people up by saying something like, "I have a story that I'm going to use in a pitch, tell me what you think?" Instead, tell the story without announcing that you are going to tell it so that you can get their natural reactions.

RESOURCES

Folk and Fairy Tales

Believe it or not, these can be some of the best sources of stories. The story about the wealthy man and the homebuilder is a folk tale that has been handed down from generation to generation.

Books

Whether fiction or nonfiction, books are an excellent source of stories.

The Media

You can get many ideas from television and movies. One of our construction management clients used the movie *Field of Dreams* as a metaphor for confirming the owner's vision for a new resort hotel. He concluded his presentation by paraphrasing the famous line in the film when he said, "Let us build it and they will come."

Famous People

Because there is so much biographical information written, stories about famous people are excellent choices. The Nixon-Kennedy debate, which I related in Chapter 1, helped make the point about the importance of appearance.

Your Own Life

This is one of the best sources of stories. Naturally, you'll want to incorporate stories (i.e., case studies) about working with clients and prospects. In addition, many of your everyday experiences make excellent stories to include in your pitches. Look for stories that occurred:

- With your spouse or significant other
- With your children or grandchildren
- In restaurants
- While traveling
- In hotels
- On vacations
- While attending sporting events

KEEP RECORDS

Whenever a story takes place in your life, write it down. Don't think about how you might use it in the future. Create a filing system—in file folders or on your computer—and save your stories by subject.

As I mentioned earlier, I carry a little alphabetized gray book in my briefcase. Every time I have an experience that is meaningful, I write the story down in my little gray book. As an example, under the letter *A*, I have stories about adulthood, attitude, airlines, and accounting. Under the letter *C*, there are stories about cities, a chef, coincidence, customer service, change, communication, coaching, challenge, character, church, children, and the cold. When I prepare a pitch, I always get out my little gray book and turn to the appropriate section to see what stories I might be able to use.

12

QUICK!
SAY SOMETHING FUNNY

How many times do you laugh a day? Five times, 10, 20, 50? Gene Perret in his book, *How to Hold Your Audience with Humor,* found that the average person laughed about 15 times a day, and participants in our audiences confirmed this. But here's the real kicker: our physiological requirement is a full five minutes of laughter a day. Clearly, we are significantly deprived in an important area of communication.

One of the biggest challenges we have in working with clients is getting them to lighten up. Most people are too serious, which results in pitches that are somber. It's as if they take to heart W.C. Fields's advice, "Start out every day with a laugh and get it out of the way." As I mentioned in Chapter 8, people don't use humor in their pitches because of the fear of failure. They'll tell us "I'm not funny" or "I can't tell a joke." Perhaps you feel this way, too.

But, as presenters, we have a mission to accomplish. It's up to us to help our audiences laugh so that they will receive their physiological requirement of at least five minutes of laughter a day.

DEVELOP YOUR SENSE OF HUMOR

The first step in using humor in our pitches is to ensure that we have a heightened sense of humor. Here are some steps to make it happen for you.

Adopt a Playful Attitude

Suppose you get in your car one morning to go to work and your car won't start. You check to be sure you have gas in tank. You turn the key again and again, but nothing happens. Frustrated, you call AAA, a towing service, or your local garage. After you've described your situation, the service attendant may ask you a pointed question, "What does it sound like?" In other words, when you turn on the ignition, what sound does the engine in your automobile make? Here's a sign in a service station I once visited when my car wouldn't budge:

Garage Sign

```
OUR  NEW  RATE
IF YOUR CAR SOUNDS LIKE - - -
PING  CLICK PING    -  $ 10.00
CLICK  WHINE CLICK  -    25.00
CLUNK  WHINE  CLUNK -    50.00
THUD  CLUNK  THUD   -   100.00
CLANG  THUD  CLANG -    300.00
CAN'T DESCRIBE IT  -    500.00
```

Everyone in this service station, from the owner to the mechanics, had a playful attitude. As I waited the 45 minutes it took them to repair my car, I could tell that the people who worked in this garage enjoyed working there.

Pike Place Fish Market in Seattle, Washington, has become famous for the philosophy of bringing fun to the workplace. Every day, thousands of locals and tourists flock to this almost nine-acre

Pike Place Fish Market

fish market located on the waterfront next to the first Starbucks store. They come not only for the quality of the product, but to watch the fish fly.

The concept of adopting a playful attitude has become so popular that Pike Place Fish Market has spawned numerous books on the subject, including *Catch! A Fishmonger's Guide to Greatness,* by Cyndi Crother, and two books by Stephen C. Lundin, Harry Paul, and John Christensen, *Fish! A Remarkable Way to Boost Morale and Improve Results* and *Fish! Sticks: A Remarkable Way to Adapt to Changing Times and Keep Your Work Fresh.* I encourage you to develop this same kind of playful attitude for yourself, your business, and your pitches.

Think Funny

The second step in developing your sense of humor is to look for the humor in everyday life. For example, take this sign.

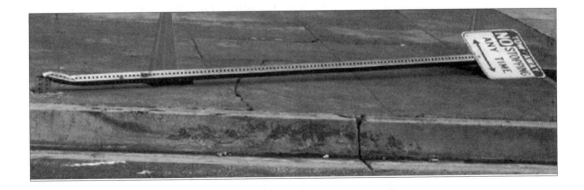

You may be saying to yourself, "What's funny about that sign?" Notice that the sign reads "No Stopping," and that some driver ran the sign over, flattening it to the ground. The humor lies in the fact that the driver obeyed the sign.

As you conduct your daily activities, be on the alert for the humor in everything around you. Pay close attention to your surroundings. I imagine that most people walked by the No Stopping sign and didn't even notice it. When you stop to examine the ordinary events of the day, you'll be surprised at how funny some of them are. It is then that you will be learning how to think funny.

Laugh at Yourself

One of the defining characteristics of powerful presenters and leaders is the ability to laugh at themselves. Unfortunately, some people have such fragile egos that they can't tolerate having someone laugh at them, much less laughing at themselves. There is no way you will be able to develop your sense of humor unless you can laugh at yourself.

Former U.S. President Bill Clinton knew how to do this. In his State of the Union speech on January 27, 2000, he used the wrong word about 2/3 of the way through his speech:

Last year the Vice President launched a new effort to make communities more liberal—livable—[laughter]—liberal, I know. [Laughter] Wait a minute, I've got a punch line now. That's this year's agenda; last year was livable, right? [Laughter] That's what Senator Lott is going to say in the commentary afterwards—[laughter]—to make our communities more livable.

President Clinton's quick wit and ability to laugh at himself made this one of his best performances.

HUMOR TARGETS

There are numerous groups and individuals you can select to have fun with. Here are some of them.

Conflict Figures

Former U. S. President Ronald Reagan used humor extremely effectively in the presidential debate with Walter Mondale on October 28, 1984. One of the panelists, Henry Trewhitt, the diplomatic correspondent for *The Baltimore Sun*, asked President Reagan, the oldest U.S. president in history, if there were any doubt in his mind that he would be able to function in a time of an international crisis.

Here's what Reagan said, "Not at all, Mr. Trewhitt. I want you to know that also I will not make age an issue of this campaign. I am not going to exploit for political purposes my opponent's youth and inexperience."

Following the debate, President Reagan's age never again became a campaign issue. This would not have been the case if Reagan answered the question in a serious manner. Imagine the reaction if he had said, "I want you to know that the Surgeon General has certified that I'm in top condition," or, "Age should never be a criteria for selecting presidents." The political pressure would only have intensified.

Reagan-Mondale Debate

The appropriate use of humor will reduce stress whenever you find yourself in conflict with another individual, be it a client, prospect, or team member. When people laugh with you, the issues become less important and, in some cases, they will go away.

Your Audience

Frequently, there will be people in your audience that you can have fun with. Of course, you want to have fun *with* them—never at their expense. They may be people you know well or those you know enjoy a good laugh.

The president of Monrovia Growers, a large wholesale grower of high quality plants, is a good example. Bruce Usrey has a tremendous sense of humor, and whenever I make a presentation to him and his senior management team, I have fun with him. Without a doubt, humor has strengthened our relationship.

Yourself

Not only should you learn to laugh at yourself as a way of developing your sense of humor, use yourself as a humor target in your presentations. Doing so makes you more human—it's an admission that you, like the people in your audience, aren't perfect. Moreover, you'll find that poking fun at yourself will build rapport between you and the audience.

Superiority Figures

Your boss or team leader can be an excellent humor target. Of course, you'll want to be sure he or she can take the humor. Pass if there's any question about this at all. However, when used appropriately, humor will enhance your relationship.

ELEMENTS OF HUMOR

Delivery

There are two components of delivery: the set up and the punch line. Let's examine both in the following joke.

There are three surprises when you get to heaven. Who's there, who's not there, and that you're there.

The set up is comprised of what you say prior to the last line "that you're there." The last line is the punch line. In many cases, there will be a punch word, as in the following:

A highway patrolman pulled a car over that was going 20 miles per hour in a 55 mile per hour zone.

"Do you know how fast you were going, ma'am?" asked the patrolmen of the elderly woman.

"Why yes, officer, 20 miles per hour. Is there anything wrong with that?" asked the woman.

"The speed limit is 55, ma'am," replied the patrolman.

"But, officer," said the woman, "the sign says 22."

"Yes, ma'am," the officer responded patiently, "that's the highway sign." With that the officer looked in the back seat to see two horrified elderly women with their mouths agape. "What happened to them?" asked the patrolman.

"We just got off of Highway 110," said the woman.

The punch word is "110" and all the other words in the joke comprise the set up.

Henny Youngman

Timing

Ninety percent of humor is timing. If your timing is off, there is no humor. Henny Youngman was one of the most famous stand-up comedians of post-vaudeville America. Columnist Walter Winchell dubbed him "the king of the one-liners," a tribute to Youngman's rapid-fire style. One of his most famous lines relied heavily on the pause: "Take my wife . . . please!"

Surprise

If the audience can guess where you're going with a joke or humorous story, your material will not be nearly as funny. Charlie Chaplin was a master at using surprise. In one of his bits, he is walking down the street, not paying attention to where he is going. In front of him is a manhole with the cover off. Instead of falling in the manhole as we would expect, at the last moment he steps over the manhole. But, that's not the surprise. When his foot comes down on the other side of the manhole, he steps on a banana peel, loses his balance, and falls. Although this type of slapstick comedy isn't as popular today as it was in Chaplin's time, Chaplin mastered the use of surprise.

Charlie Chaplin

GUIDELINES FOR USING HUMOR

Wait to Laugh at Your Own Material

Perhaps you've seen people tell a joke during a presentation and, before they get to the punch line, they begin laughing. This can be annoying to the people who are listening. The audience wants to get to the punch line so they can laugh, too. Moreover, laughing before you get to punch line can make you look silly if no one laughs after you've delivered the punch line. You'll leave the audience wondering what was so funny. So, wait until you say the punch line, then laugh with the audience.

Let the Audience Laugh

Have you ever seen a presenter tell a joke and, as the audience is laughing, go on with his next point? When you continue speaking as soon as you deliver the punch line, you may stifle the laughter. Let the audience enjoy the laugh; remember, we need five full minutes of laughter a day. As importantly, if you continue speaking as people are laughing, they won't hear what you're saying.

Never Laugh at People, Laugh with Them

Laughing at people in your audience could create friction and animosity. Instead, when you say something funny, enjoy a laugh with people. The idea is to have fun with the audience, not at its expense.

Acknowledge Groaners

A groaner is a joke you tell that, for whatever reason, the audience doesn't think is funny. I'm sure this has happened to you before. You tell a joke to someone and instead of laughing, she groans. Groaners occur due to one or more of the following:

- You didn't deliver the joke well
- Your timing was off
- The punch line was obvious
- The joke wasn't funny

Johnny Carson

When you use humor in presentations, expect some occasional groaners and be prepared for them. Have some responses ready that acknowledge to the audience that your attempt at humor wasn't successful. You might say something like, "When I told that joke to my 80-year-old grandmother last night, it really cracked her up," or, "My five-year-old daughter thought that was the funniest joke she'd ever heard, I don't know what went wrong."

Johnny Carson regularly acknowledged groaners during his 30 years as host of the *Tonight Show*. Frequently, he would blame the groaners on his writers, who he threatened to fire if they didn't come up with better material.

If You Bomb, Keep Going

You might tell a joke or use what you consider a humorous line and people won't laugh or groan. This is not the time for you to act like a stand up comic and say something like, "This must not be a very sharp group. That was a joke." Comments like this will create animosity and place a barrier between you and the audience. Instead, keep going. Act like you had just made a serious point.

In a pitch I gave one Monday morning, I used several funny lines and stories to lighten up my presentation. To my surprise, no one laughed after each of my humor attempts. Nonetheless, I continued on as if the funny lines and stories were meant to be serious. Afterward, several people came up to me and told me how much they appreciated the information I had given them. Not one said anything about my failed attempt to use humor. I'm sure they thought I had given an excellent serious presentation.

Make the Dialogue Live

As with stories, use dialogue in jokes to create animation. Don't merely refer to conversations that characters in your jokes have. For maximum effect, always create the dialogue just as if the audience were listening to a live performance.

Keep It Brief

William Shakespeare had it right when he said, "Brevity is the sole of wit." Many a joke are destroyed by too many words, as in the following set up:

Several years ago a man drove from Atlanta to Washington, DC, to see friends. It was a long, hot day, so he decided to stop in a small town in North Carolina and have a beer. He parked his car in front of a bar and put a quarter in the parking machine. As he entered the bar, he noticed an empty stool at the bar. When he sat down, the bartender came over to him and asked, "What'll it be, buddy?"

The joke would be much better by omitting the unnecessary information about the trip and by beginning with the following:

The bartender leaned over to the man and asked "What'll it be, buddy?"

Remove all the unnecessary words, phrases, and descriptions and watch how much stronger your jokes become.

Practice on Everyone

As with stories, never tell a joke for the first time in a pitch. Practice your jokes on friends and family members to be sure you have the delivery and timing down. You'll get a truer reaction if you don't set them up by prefacing your joke with "I have a funny joke that I'm working on for a presentation, tell me how you like it." Just tell the joke as part of your conversation with people to get their natural reactions.

Listen for the Laughs

You can add humor to your presentation by doing what the professionals do. Record and listen to your presentations, then pay attention to where the audiences laugh. Keep the lines that get you the laughs. You'll be surprised at how much of your humor is spontaneous.

I had the privilege of presenting an award to Bob Hope some years back. Bob was hilarious in giving his acceptance speech, and the audience responded in nonstop laughter. Afterward, he asked me, "What did I say that got the laugh after you placed the medallion around my neck? I have to remember that one." His manager, Ward Grant, who was standing next to me, knew exactly what he had said and made a note of the comment.

POTENTIAL SOURCES

Joke Books

Many professional comics have written books containing their favorite jokes. These books are excellent sources of material for your jokes. But don't merely use the jokes you get from these books, use a technique professionals call "joke-switching." Take the set up from one joke and switch it with a punch line from another joke that is appropriate for the audience.

I used the following joke I found in a joke book for a speech I gave at a retreat for a major accounting firm. Here's how the original joke goes:

> One day God and Satan had a battle for power. God said, "Let there be light." And there was light, and it was good. God turned to Satan and exclaimed, "Top that!" Satin thought for a moment and commanded, "Let there be politicians!"

I did some joke-switching with this joke to reflect the sanctions being placed upon accountants by the government as a result of fraudulent activities of such companies as Enron, World-Com, and Tyco. When I used the joke for the accountants, I replaced the punch word *politicians* with *regulators*.

The Internet

There are numerous humor Web sites you can access for a wealth of jokes and one-liners. Many will e-mail you jokes daily. Please see the Resources section for a listing of helpful humor Web sites.

Professional Comics

You can get great jokes and ideas for ways to include humor in your pitches by observing stand up comedians on television and in live performances. Cable television offers several hours of stand up programming daily. Most cities have comedy clubs where local comics perform nightly. Not only is this a fun way to spend your evening, you'll be doing research at the same time.

Personal Experiences

Some of the funny experiences you have had with your family, friends, and associates are excellent humorous stories you can use in your pitches. I love to use stories about my daughter. Not only have we had many funny things happen to us, she has a wonderful sense of humor.

One day we were on our way to a cross-town library to return some books. I thought it would be fun to have a picnic while we were there, so I packed some sandwiches. After we'd returned the books, I said to Gabi, "OK, let's go have our picnic." To my surprise Gabi replied, "Let's eat the sandwiches in the car. There's going to be a TV show on that I want to watch, so I want to get home right away."

Because I was the driver, I prevailed. As we sat down to enjoy our sandwiches, I decided I would talk to Gabi about the importance of enjoying life and not always being in such a hurry. "Gabi, isn't it beautiful here?"

"Yes," replied Gabi.

"Aren't you glad we decided to have our picnic instead of eating in the car?" I continued.

"No," she said flatly.

"Gabi," I said. "You have to learn to stop and smell the roses. Do you know what that means?"

She thought for a moment and said, "No."

"That means that you shouldn't always be in such a hurry that you don't enjoy life. Sometimes people are so busy that they don't even stop to notice flowers," I explained.

Without missing a beat, Gabi said, "I'd rather go home and smell the TV."

When she said that, I burst out laughing. Then she started laughing. Soon we were both laughing so loud that people at the surrounding picnic tables were looking at us with quizzical expressions.

I have told that story many times to reinforce the point that what's important to one person may not be to another. Every time I tell it, I get a chuckle. I'm sure you have similar humorous experiences you can share with clients and prospects. Not only do personal experiences allow you to reinforce your points, they humanize you and draw you closer to your audience.

Avoid Using Other People's Humor

Most presenters have signature humorous stories. These are the stories that they have crafted using the sources we just discussed. Never use their material, no matter how great the laugh was that they received. Come up with your own material. It's not that hard, and then it will be uniquely yours.

KEEP RECORDS

Just as I suggested in Chapter 11, record the good jokes you hear immediately. They will be a wonderful source of joke-switching. Similarly, record the humorous experiences you have for easy reference when you organize your next pitch. Include the painful and unpleasant experiences, too. They may be your funniest stories in the future.

As you know, I use my little gray book. Whether you record jokes and experiences in a book or on a computer, do it. Don't rely on your memory.

13

THE SECRETS OF BUILDING RAPPORT

Having completed my firm's securities training program four months prior, I was excited about the important pitch I was about to make. Seated in the room were 100 of Beverly Hills's most wealthy investors. I had hand-delivered personal invitations to each one of the men and women in the audience, requesting their attendance at the Beverly Wilshire Hotel to hear my seminar "Sophisticated Investment Strategies of the Decade."

At 7:00 PM, I walked to the front of the room, got the audience's attention, and launched into my presentation. After I had been speaking for no more than five minutes, a gentleman on the right side, about four rows back, raised his hand. Marveling how someone might have a question this early in the seminar, I asked, "Yes, sir, do you have a question?"

With that, the man stood up and said, "Mr. Hankins, we . . . ," and he gestured broadly to include the other people in room, "came here this evening to hear about sophisticated investment strategies. We have been sitting here patiently for the last five minutes, and we have yet to hear you say one, single sophisticated word." The man continued to stand as the stunned audience silently awaited my response. At the back of the room was a large silver bowl filled with bottled soft drinks and ice. So quiet was the room that you could hear the ice melting against the bottles.

I had just received an objection, and a *hostile* objection at that. Objections, if not handled well, can turn an otherwise excellent pitch into a disaster. Not only do we run the risk of losing control of the audience, but, more importantly, losing the business.

In this chapter, we'll discuss the vital steps you must take to build rapport with any audience, including a powerful strategy you can use to rehearse responses to the most challenging questions. And don't worry; I won't forget to tell you what happened to me at the Beverly Wilshire Hotel.

THE READY POSITION

The first step in preparing yourself for a powerful pitch is to get in the ready position: you must be mentally and physically prepared.

Mentally

The audience doesn't care that you are so excited about the presentation that you only got three hours of sleep, that you almost had an automobile accident on the way to the meeting, or that you have a cold. The audience expects that you'll be totally focused, present, and upbeat. You must be mentally prepared.

The New England Patriots taught us about the importance of attitude when they won Super Bowl XXXVI in 2002. At the beginning of the season, everyone thought the Patriots would do poorly. That is, everyone except the New England Patriots. What people didn't know is that the team had something more than talent and experience; they had a very positive attitude. Adam Vinatieri, who kicked the winning field goal, helped us to understand the team's winning attitude during his post game interview.

> Interviewer: "Congratulations!"
>
> Adam Vinatieri: "Thank you. Thank you very much."
>
> Interviewer: "What's it feel like?"
>
> Adam Vinatieri: "Everybody played so well today. We went out there and showed the world we're the best team out there."
>
> Interviewer: "What can you say about shocking people?"
>
> Adam Vinatieri: "You know what? This team believed that we had it. We didn't think we were underdogs. We deserved a chance to win this. We just proved to the world that we're the best."

One of the reasons the Patriots won is because they got it right mentally. They believed they could win. Throughout their training camps and into the season, their collective conscious mind convinced their subconscious mind. Every player reaffirmed the belief before each game they played.

My experience is that frequently people are not as mentally prepared. I once coached a man for an out-of-town presentation he was to give to a large group of investors the next morning. As I arrived at the meeting location, my client approached me in a frazzled, almost exhausted condition.

"Gary," he said, "I don't think I can do it."

"What's the matter?" I asked.

"I didn't sleep at all last night," he replied. "I tossed and turned as I thought about what I was going to say today. To make matters worse, the bed was hard and my pillow was lumpy. I feel like s—!"

I placed my hands on his shoulders, looked into his eyes and said, "Here's what I want you to do. I want you to image that you had a great night's sleep. Don't think about how you didn't sleep.

Think only about how well you did sleep. Forget about how tired you feel. From this point on, you feel rejuvenated, rested, and ready for your presentation. Got it?"

"Got it," he answered as a sense of calm came over him.

Thirty minutes later, he made one of the best pitches of his life. The exercise I took him through is the same one you can do for yourself if you are not mentally ready. It's as if you must play a mental trick on yourself when you find yourself in a less than optimum condition. The best thing you can do for yourself is to tell your subconscious mind that you feel great and that you're ready to make a powerful pitch.

Physically

You must take care of the physical plant: the body. Preparing for, giving, and following up on pitches takes a lot of stamina. It's vital that you be in good physical condition. Exercise regularly; it will increase your stamina. Recently one of my friends and a highly successful agent at Northwestern Mutual Life, Dave Meschulam, informed me that he was going to swim an hour every morning for the next 30 days. "Why such a rigorous regimen?" I asked. "Well," replied Dave, "I have a lot of work coming up over the next month and I want to be sure I have the energy to see it completed successfully."

Be sure to drink plenty of water on a daily basis as a great way to control your weight, improve digestion, and keep your skin tones. A gallon a day works wonders.

The evening before your presentation, eat easily digestible foods that are not going to cause you to toss and turn all night long. Skip the spicy foods and eat lighter than you might normally. Don't stay up late enhancing your pitch—you'll place your mind in a working mode that may be impossible to turn off. Go to bed early and get enough sleep.

The morning of the presentation, eat a high-protein break-fast. You'll need plenty of energy. Have a protein bar ready in case you don't have time for breakfast. Another good idea is to keep a supply of nuts handy. They're a quick solution for high protein and an excellent way to keep your energy level up throughout the day. I once asked a man who had worked with motivational speaker Tony Robbins how Tony keep his energy up for 12 to 14 hours a day, sometimes for three days in a row. He told me that Tony usually takes a short break every hour or so. When he does, he goes backstage and pops a handful of almonds in his mouth.

If you have milk, cream, or yogurt the morning of your presentation, you will frequently need to clear you throat. Dairy products cause phlegm, and you don't need this irritation. Cut the dairy.

You also should avoid coffee because it will dry out your throat. Have a glass of water handy at the presentation to keep your throat moist.

BEFORE THE MEETING STARTS

Arrive Early

Get to the room thirty minutes before the first person arrives. Check the room setup—make sure seating, temperature and lighting is as you wish. If you're using audiovisual equipment, arrive an hour early. Check the equipment to be sure it's working properly. You can count on there being challenges. You want to have it working smoothly before people enter the room.

Arriving early gives you an opportunity to meet the audience members as they arrive. Not only does this help you build rapport, it gets you onstage and prepares you for a strong introduction.

I got on an elevator recently with another man who turned to me and said, "You're Gary Hankins."

Somewhat surprised, I replied, "Yes. Have we met?"

He said, "Well, yes. We met briefly. I was at a conference that you spoke at in Las Vegas a few years ago, and I'll never forget you."

Now, this is the type of comment ever professional speaker loves to hear. "Really?" I asked, "Tell me more about that."

"Well," he answered, "I liked your program. But, the big takeaway for me was not what you said in your presentation."

Now I was really curious. "Really?" I asked.

"What I remember most about you," he continued, "is that you stood at the door and shook hands with every one of the 500 people that came in the room that morning. I've never seen anybody do that at any conference before or since. And I noticed what it did for you. Everybody felt as if they knew you when you started to speak. You built instant rapport. I liked this idea so much that now, every time I speak, I use it myself."

Although I was somewhat concerned that the content of my program wasn't more memorable, his comments validated the importance of meeting people as they arrive.

Sometimes it may not be possible to get into the room before your audience. This might be the case in a "beauty contest" where you're one of a number of people or teams chosen to present to a selection committee during the day. In the case where another person or group is presenting before you, be prepared to enter the room as soon as the previous presentation is over. Of course, you won't have this challenge if yours is the first presentation of the day.

Create the Moment

Before you begin your pitch, be sure that everyone is quiet and looking at you before you say a word. If you start speaking while other people in the room are having conversations, you won't have their attention and, in larger audiences, you may never get it. Silence is a powerful attention-getting technique.

Creating the moment can be a particular challenge when you host a cocktail reception for clients and prospects. After about an hour of socializing and networking, typically you will welcome the guests and make a short pitch about your company. Usually you will find yourself speaking to the people gathered immediately around you. Meanwhile, there are usually other people in the room continuing to carry on conversations.

A great way to be sure that you get everyone's attention is to tap a spoon against a wine glass—the universal "be quiet, please" signal. It works every time. Then, when everyone in the room is quiet and paying attention, begin your presentation. Pitches you give at receptions that you host are tremendous opportunities to persuade prospects to do business with you. Be sure you have the full attention of every person in the room.

Create a Customized Introduction

Whenever possible, have someone introduce you. It will sound better coming from someone other than you. Provide introducers with a customized introduction in advance of the meeting so that they don't choose for themselves what they think is most important. Your introduction should address the following points:

- Why this topic
- Why you
- Why now

Use a standard size paper with 14 point type. Write at the top of the page "Please read exactly as written." You don't want people ad-libbing—they'll usually mess it up. Don't mention your name until the end. This creates the same dramatic impact that Ed

McMahon gave Johnny Carson on the *Tonight Show* when he would say, "And here's Johnny!" The following introduction will give you a good idea of the layout.

Keynote Introduction for GARY HANKINS

(Please read exactly as written)

GOOD AFTERNOON!

IT'S A PLEASURE FOR ME TO INTRODUCE OUR SPEAKER. HE'S AN INTERNATIONAL KEYNOTE SPEAKER, AUTHOR, COACH, AND PRESIDENT OF PYGMALION.

PRIOR TO FOUNDING PYGMALION, HE WAS A TOP PRODUCER IN THE COMPETITIVE SECURITIES INDUSTRY. AS A STOCK-BROKER, HE BUILT HIS BUSINESS BY GIVING INVESTMENT SEMINARS, HOSTING HIS OWN RADIO AND TELEVISION SHOWS, AND PUBLISHING A NEWSLETTER.

THEN 15 YEARS AGO, HE REALIZED HIS PASSION WAS SPEAKING AND NOT INVESTING MONEY FOR PEOPLE, AND THAT HIS CALLING IN LIFE WAS TO HELP OTHER PEOPLE BECOME POWERFUL COMMUNICATORS.

HIS CLIENTS INCLUDE JONES LANG LASALLE, DELOITTE & TOUCHE, BAXTER BIOSCIENCE, THE YOUNG PRESIDENTS ORGANIZATION, THE NATIONAL FOOTBALL LEAGUE, THE ATLANTA FALCONS, AND THE SAN FRANCISCO 49ERS.

THIS AFTERNOON HE WILL TALK WITH US ABOUT "THE POWER OF THE PITCH."

LET'S GIVE A BIG WELCOME TO . . . GARY HANKINS!

THE POWER OF TEAM DYNAMICS

If you give team presentations, audiences will observe you to see how you function as a team and what it would be like to work with your team. The audience's perception of your team dynamics will play a chief role in determining whether or not you get the business. Incorporate the following steps in your team pitches and you'll do well.

Be Here Now

What takes place frequently in team presentations is that the team members who are not speaking don't pay attention to the team member who is speaking. The nonspeaking team members often look bored or disinterested, which models behavior for the audience. If your teammates aren't interested, why should the audience be?

The president of a company was invited to be part of the presentation team for an important pitch to beat four competitors for a large outsourcing assignment. At the appropriate moment, the president stood up and said, "I wanted to be here today to tell you how important you will be to us as a client." He made some additional comments and ended by pledging the full support of the organization. He then sat down at the other end of the conference table, opened up his laptop, and spent the remainder of the meeting doing some personal work.

When the team leader conducted the audience debriefing after learning that the business was given to a competitor, she was told that the prospective client was so incensed by her president's disrespectful behavior that the prospect dismissed her company from further consideration. What a surprise. The president might as well have said, "I have other matters that are more important than this meeting, but the team insisted that I be here."

The reaction of your team is just as important. Perhaps you've been in the situation where your teammates seem disinterested in what you're saying. Not only is it demoralizing, it's rude. Your team must be totally present. The consulting firm of Senn-Delaney has an excellent expression, "Be here now." The idea is to be in the moment and to put all distractions aside. Attentive behavior on the part of your team builds individual confidence and team spirit. Importantly, it says to the audience, "If these people are that interested in what they're saying in this meeting, I should be, too."

The Seamless Transition

When teams transition from one team member to another, they usually use "the handoff." The handoff occurs when one team member finishes his presentation and hands it off to another. If it were a pitch given by an advertising agency, the first presenter might conclude her part of the pitch with something like, "We urge you to engage us to create a consistent brand image for you that will allow you to dominate the market. I'll now turn it over to Greg Smith who will talk to you about the budget." Greg comes up and says, "Thank you very much, Sally. I'm going to cover the proposed budget with you." The handoff is trite, time consuming, and often awkward.

The seamless transition avoids the hand off. Using the advertising agency example, Sally finishes her presentation with, "We urge you to engage us to create a consistent brand image for you that will allow you to dominate the market." Sally then moves to the side and Greg steps up and says, "Creating a consistent brand image that will allow you to dominate the market could conservatively double your revenues over the next 12 months. We've created a budget at fraction of this revenue goal."

The seamless transition is a smooth way to easily move from one presenter to the next. When it's your turn to speak, stand up close to the front of the room so there's no delay. If there's a lapse in time, it's not going to be seamless. Of course, be sure to practice the seamless transition in your rehearsals.

THE ART OF ASKING QUESTIONS

Asking questions of the audience is one of the best ways to build rapport. Can you image pitches in which there are no questions? Prospects or clients merely sit there passively and listen to you. Given this scenario, it is extremely unlikely that your pitch will be successful. Conversely, the more interaction you have with the audience, the better. When you make a pitch, you are building a relationship with people. Here's how it works: the greater the level of communication, the stronger the relationship, the higher are the probabilities of success.

The 20-50-80 Principle

The purpose of asking questions is to be sure that people are paying attention and understand what you're telling them. If people aren't listening or don't understand what you're saying, you've lost them. If asked only 30 minutes after your presentation, they won't remember what you said.

Remember, when people either hear or see a message, their retention of that information is about 20 percent. When they hear *and* see, retention goes up to 50 percent. This is one of the chief reasons for including visual aids in your presentation. But, when people hear, see, and do, their retention jumps to 80 percent. One of the best activities you can have an audience do is to ask and answer questions.

The 20-50-80 Principle

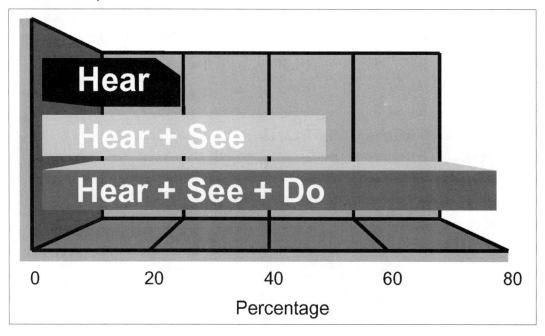

Practice Empathetic Listening

When you ask a question, focus all of your attention on the answer someone gives to you. Perhaps you've seen something like this happen on a television interview. The camera is on the host as he asks a question of his guest, "Tell me, what was you childhood like." A second camera now picks up the guest who answers the question. What we don't see is what the host is doing. Frequently, the host studies his list of questions to see what he is going to ask next while the guest answers the question. On occasion, the guest finishes his answer with an unpredicted statement, such as, "And so, out of shear frustration, I axe murdered my mother." To which the host responds, "That's great. Now I notice in your book that . . ."

This act of not listening to answers occurs in presentations every day. It says to the people who are listening to your pitch, "Why should I answer a question? She doesn't care anyway." If there is no care—no empathy—people will not participate. If they don't participate, you will not establish a relationship with them and they won't buy.

Remember the Question

Another reason for practicing empathetic listening is to be sure the listener answers the question. Politicians will frequently not answer the question posed to them. If the response doesn't address your question, ask it again.

Avoid Rhetorical Questions

A rhetorical question is one that doesn't need an answer or one that you answer yourself. Remember that one of the chief reasons for asking questions is to build rapport. If you answer questions yourself, it says to the listener, "I don't need to pay attention. I can dream about my vacation to Hawaii." Chances are most people would rather be sprawled out on a beach towel in Hawaii than sitting in a hard seat in a room with no windows listening to you. If you don't involve them, they will be on the beach. If you leave them on the beach, the only thing they'll buy is another piña colada.

Ask the question and wait for a response. If no one answers, ask the question again in a different manner. Perhaps your first question was unclear. Now, if no one answers, call on someone who looks like they're paying attention and have the answer. The signal you are sending by asking questions in this manner is that you want the audience involved in the presentation. It changes the dynamics of the meeting. Your subliminal message is, "I'm not speaking *to* you, I'm speaking *with* you and I expect you to take an active role in this meeting."

Welcome All Answers

Occasionally, you'll ask a question and someone will respond with an answer that indicates he or she hasn't been paying attention to you. Don't get upset. Be kind. Be gentle. Remember, this could happen to you. The person who answered incorrectly knows that he or she momentarily drifted off. By treating people respectfully, you'll receive the admiration of the individual as well as everyone else in the audience.

THE ART OF ANSWERING QUESTIONS

Encourage Questions Throughout

Not only do you want to ask questions of the audience, you want people to ask you questions. Sometimes you'll need to encourage people to participate. In the early part of your presentation, say something like, "Let's make this a valuable experience today. Anytime you have any questions or comments, please let me know."

Acknowledge the Inquirer

Instead of just answering the question, first tell people that you appreciate their asking questions. Appropriate responses include "Thank you for that question," "I appreciate that question," or "I'm glad you asked that question."

Be careful not to evaluate the question. If you respond with "Great question" or "Excellent question," how will someone feel when you don't rate that person's question? If the previous question received an "excellent" response and this one a mere "thank you," the questioner is likely to think, "I thought my question was better than the previous question. Why was his excellent and mine wasn't?"

Repeat the Question If Necessary

You may need to repeat the question if you are presenting to a large audience, or if you're audio- or videotaping your presentation. Otherwise, don't repeat the question, as the audience will see this as a stalling technique to allow you think of the answer. The perception will be a diminished depth of knowledge on your part.

Answer the Question If It's Appropriate

There are three situations in which you would not want to answer a question:

- If you are going to cover the topic later in your presentation. If so, ask the questioner to hold the question until then.
- If the question doesn't relate to your topic. If so, ask the questioner to see you after your presentation, at which time you would be pleased to answer the question.
- If the question is of such specific interest that others in the audience wouldn't be interested. In this case, table it for another time. In a recent presentation, the IT presenter took a question from the IT person on the prospect's team that was so technical the two of them got into a 20-minute discussion that lost everyone else at the meeting.

Don't Embarrass

Sometime during the course of your presentation someone may ask you a question on a topic or point that you previously discussed. The question clearly indicates that he or she wasn't paying attention. Avoid the temptation to preface your answer with "As I discussed earlier." Your comment will only embarrass the person who asked you the question. Just answer the question as if you'd never covered the point before. The questioner may not notice how you handle the situation, but other people will, and they'll admire you for your sensitivity.

Don't Bluff

This can be a challenge, especially if you're just starting in your profession. You might feel that it's better to make information up rather than to look stupid in the eyes of your audience. Don't fall into this trap. If you don't know the answer to a question, admit it. The audience won't expect you to have all the answers. When you don't know the answer, say something like, "I appreciate that question. Unfortunately, I'm not familiar with that issue, but I'd be happy to research it for you and give you a call tomorrow."

Being honest is the best strategy. One word of caution: telling people you don't know the answer to difficult questions will work fine for a few times. However, if you have to admit your lack of knowledge to questions repeatedly throughout your presentation, the audience will come to the correct conclusion that you're not well informed. Remember our discussion in Chapter 7, before you think about making a presentation, be sure you know your topic cold.

Answer the Question for Everyone

When someone asks you a question, be sure to focus your attention on that person. When you answer the question, answer it for everyone in the room, not just for the person who asked it. Perhaps you've seen the presenter and someone in the audience enter into a conversation that excludes everyone else. Not only does this show a lack of consideration for other people, it is a great way to lose control of the audience.

Begin your answer by acknowledging the questioner and then answer the question by moving your eye contact at two- to four-second intervals from one person to the next, including the questioner. This way, everyone feels included.

Answer the Question and Be Quiet

Perhaps you've noticed that some presenters go on and on with their answers. They answer the question, and then they answer the question again with slight modifications, and they may even answer the question one last time. Answer the question and be quiet. If the person asking the question needs clarification, he or she will ask you. If the questioner doesn't ask for clarification, but you can tell by the person's nonverbal expressions that he or she wasn't satisfied with your answer, ask if you adequately addressed the question.

A word of caution: avoid the strategy of checking with the person who asked you a question if you are making a pitch to a large audience. Recently, I attended a meeting at which a woman made a pitch about her company to an audience of about 100 people. During the question and answer period, she answered a question from a man in the back of the room. When she completed her answer, she said to the man, "I can tell by your facial expression that

I may not have answered your question." He said, "No, you didn't," and rephrased his question. So she answered the question again with some modifications. Noticing his apparent displeasure with her response, she again asked if she had addressed his question. At this point, other people in the audience had entered into conversations. Some were leaving the room. As she answered the question for a third time, about 20 people in the room got up and left. The others had become disinterested.

If you want to get a good lesson on how to answer questions to a large audience, watch President George W. Bush's next press conference. The President will answer one question and move immediately to the next. Checking in with each person who asked the question would be disastrous.

THE FOUR STEPS TO OVERCOMING OBJECTIONS

Occasionally someone will ask you a question or make a statement with the intent of discrediting you and or your message. The pronouncement the man made at the beginning of my investment seminar clearly qualifies as an objection. Let's continue the story and see how I dealt with my rude and impatient guest. Remember, the man just said that he had yet to hear me utter one sophisticated word.

I thought for about five seconds and then asked the man a question that came to me in one of those moments of rare genius, "Tell me, sir, what did you come here to learn about this evening?"

"I came here to learn how to short stock without any risk," replied the man.

"Excellent," I said. "I will show you how to short stock and simultaneously buy a put option and thereby create a riskless transition. What else did you come here to learn about?"

"Well, I want to learn how to create a risk arbitrage portfolio in my own account," the man responded.

"That's great," I responded. "I'll show you how you to structure and manage your own risk arbitrage portfolio and produce some very attractive returns. Is there anything else you came here to learn about this evening?"

The man thought for a moment and said, "No."

As the man was sitting down, I looked around the room and noticed that quite a few people where smiling. It could have been my imagination, but I thought I saw a few people giving me a "thumbs up." You see, people want you to succeed. They want you to give a great presentation. I succeeded because I used what I have come to recognize as a powerful method for overcoming objections.

Stay Calm

Count to ten, breathe deeply, do whatever you do when you find yourself in a threatening position. You may feel vulnerable, but you don't want to show it.

Don't Argue

I could have said, "I've only been speaking for five minutes." To which the man might have replied, "Five minutes is plenty of time to say something sophisticated." I might have responded with "No, it isn't," the man with "Yes, it is," and we could have gone back and forth many times. This is a no-win situation.

Seek Specifics

Instead of arguing, I asked the question, "Tell me what you came to learn about this evening?" This simple technique of asking a question for clarification will become one of the most important tools you will use in dealing with difficult questions.

Anytime you make a pitch, you open yourself up to an objection. If you give many pitches, sooner or later somebody is going to take a shot at you. When that happens, you want to find out what's behind that question so you can have a meaningful conversation. The question you want to ask is one you perfected when you were two: "Why?" Of course, you would ask "Why?" in a conversational tone. It's not only what you say, but how you say it. Let's suppose someone makes the objection: "Your service appears to be very expensive." Your responses could include:

- "Just out of curiosity, why do you say that?
- "How so?"
- "Say more about that."
- "Tell me, what causes you to say that?"

When you seek specifics, the communication that follows will allow you to focus on the concerns that the person has. Now you can get to what's behind the objection.

The Feel-Felt-Found Formula

Once you determine the specific concerns, use this powerful formula. Let's use the fee objection as an example.

Prospect: "Your service appears to be very expensive."
You: "Just out of curiosity, what causes you say that?"
Prospect: "It's a lot more than I thought we would have to spend."
You: "How much did you think you would have to spend?"
Prospect: "Well, I thought it might be about half of what we're talking about."

You: "I understand how you *feel*. One of our clients, ABC Company, *felt* that way when we presented our proposal. Our fee was more than they had budgeted. But, what they *found* is that during the first six months of working with us, we were able to save the company five times our fee. As you can see in this letter from Bob Smith, the President of ABC, he said, 'Working with your firm was one of the most financially rewarding decisions we have ever made.'"

By using a story and a testimonial letter in the Feel-Felt-Found Formula, you offer proof that your solution is worth the fee. You'll want to have several stories or case studies at your disposal for each potential objection.

THE KILLER THREE

In every pitch you make, you will usually have three objections which, if you don't deal with them well, will kill your presentation. Keep in mind these are not polite questions people will ask you for clarification, they're questions or statements objecting to the validity of your pitch, in part or in its entirety.

Take a minute to write down the Killer Three for a pitch you give frequently.

1. _____
2. _____
3. _____

Now write down the responses to each of the Killer Three.

1. _____
2. _____
3. _____

For every pitch you make, rehearse your responses to the Killer Three with your team or others who know your business.

In this chapter, we've discussed:

- Important steps to take before the meeting starts
- The power of winning team dynamics
- The art of asking questions
- The art of answering questions
- How to overcome objections

Please review these concepts regularly. Your ability to build a relationship with the audience and overcome challenging questions is critical. By developing these key competencies, you will become more persuasive and you will win more business.

14

PICTURES ARE WORTH
A MILLION DOLLARS

One of our construction management clients conducted a debriefing of a pitch he and his team made to a large hotel chain for the construction of a new resort. The prospect told him that the reason his company chose a competitor was because of the flowchart the competitor used to describe the construction process. The prospect went on to describe how the chart showed the various steps in the process. Somewhat annoyed that the prospect could make a decision based on a chart, he pointed out that his firm had exactly the same process.

"Yes, your process was almost identical," agreed the prospect. "But, when these guys traced the various steps involved to ensure the success of our project, we got it." What the prospect said provides a valuable lesson in the power of pictures. Visual aids can play an important role in pitches. According to research conducted by the University of Minnesota and 3M Corporation, visuals can increase the likelihood that the audience will take action by 43 percent.

Armed with the knowledge that you'll be much more likely to persuade an audience if you use visual aids than if you don't, you

The Impact of AV

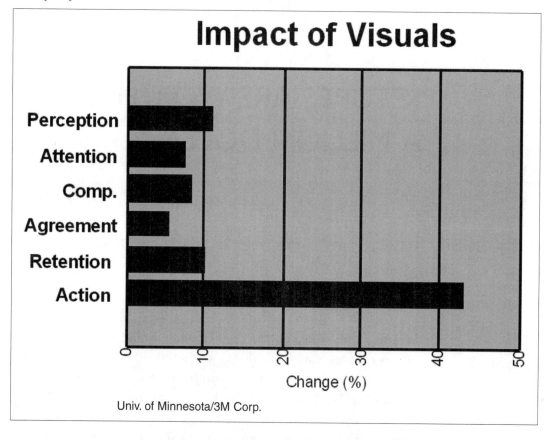

Univ. of Minnesota/3M Corp.

may be thinking that including visuals in your presentations is an easy solution to winning business. Presenters around the world have come to this conclusion, too. In response to this collective desire to win by using visual aids, software manufacturers have developed simple presentation solutions. With no more than a 30-minute tutorial, presenters can create the magic potion that will nearly assure the success of their presentations.

Herein lies the challenge. Due to the ease of use of presentation software, presenters create slides to illustrate every point. Most of those illustrations are no more than text slides that serve as an outline for the presenter. The presenter places a slide on the screen and then reads each bullet point to the audience. This is a great way to insult the intelligence of an adult. When we were young children, we liked to have our parents read to us. But that was because we didn't know how to read. Now that we do know how to read, having someone read to us is boring and aggravating.

If used improperly, audiovisuals can reduce your excellent pitch to a pile of rubble. In this chapter, we'll discuss how to keep that from happening, and, importantly, how to use visuals to make you millions.

THE PURPOSE OF VISUALS

The reason for using any visual aid in your pitch is to *better* communicate information. If the visual you're contemplating using doesn't enhance your pitch, don't use it. Don't fall into the trap of using visuals as an outline to guide you from one point to the next. Visuals are not for you; they're for the audience. Due to the misuse of presentation software, many customers and prospects are requesting that presenters not use slides. This is unfortunate because, if used properly, visuals can be a powerful tool to winning the business.

TYPES OF VISUAL AIDS

Flipcharts, White Boards, and Electronic Boards

These are excellent tools for recording the spontaneous responses from an audience. When facilitating meetings, always have one of these tools so that you can record and validate ideas and recommendations. For strategy sessions, place the pieces of flipchart paper or paper generated from an electronic board on the walls of the room for reference during the meeting.

Boards

Used frequently in the real estate and legal professions, foam-backed boards are useful when you need a high quality visual for a space unequipped for multimedia. Some types of rooms where boards are a good alternative are some courtrooms, open spaces, and rooms with a lot of sunlight. The negative to using boards is that they are expensive to make or change and are cumbersome to carry.

Computer-Driven Presentations

The laptop computer is the delivery method of choice today. It allows you to present interactive slides, animation, and video at the click of a mouse. Moreover, you can keep your presentation current by making changes to your presentation software minutes before you present.

For presentations where you're meeting with one or two people, use your laptop by itself. When you arrive in the prospect's lobby, turn on the computer, open your presentation, bring up the first slide, and close the lid. When you sit down in the conference room next to your prospect, place your laptop computer on the table in front of you and between you and the prospect. When you're ready to refer to your presentation, open up the laptop lid and away you go.

For three or more people, use an LCD (liquid crystal display) or a DLP (digital light processing) projector. As an alternative, you could use a large monitor or television.

Handouts and Flipbooks

Never give the audience anything to look at until you're ready for people to look at it. One of the challenges with using a handout or flipbook is lack of control. While you're speaking, people will flip through the pages, looking for something more interesting than what you're talking about. This means they're not listening to you.

Chances are they will turn to the last page of your proposal to see what it's going to cost. One of our clients told us of just such an occurrence. While she was discussing the key issues, the president of the company turned to the fee page and blurted out, "You've got to be kidding!" Instead of building a strong case for why the prospect needed her service, our client then had to go into defense mode. This interruption was so devastating that she never recovered and subsequently lost the business.

A handout is valuable in that it serves as reference source, but use it as a leave-behind tool. Use your laptop or projection screen for the audience to view during your pitch. Then distribute the handouts after you've concluded. Tell the audience at the beginning of your presentation not to worry about taking copious notes because all the information you present will be handed out after your presentation. If it's impractical to use a presentation software program, pass out the contents of the handout one page at a time.

Props

These are all the items you introduce into your pitch to help the audience understand or remember key points. As an example, in our workshops we ask participants to stand up and evaluate the people who have just presented. To aid in the learning process, we provide each participant with a Pygmalion mug filled with 12 marbles. When the evaluators use fillers or non-positives, the other participants drop marbles into mugs. This helps everyone become aware of the use of fillers and non-positives. In addition, we provide participants with stress balls with a big smile on them to remind people to smile frequently.

Perhaps you have had teachers who made the complex easy through the use of clever props, which they introduced at appropriate moments. One of my college professors began a class one day in a seemingly unorthodox manner. He entered the classroom, approached a table at the front of the room, and began flipping coins onto the table. He didn't say a word for about 60 seconds. All we heard was the sound of one coin after another as it landed on the table. The coins he used to grab our attention set the stage for the most memorable lecture about the U.S. monetary system in my educational experience.

Think creatively about your presentations. Always ask yourself, "What can I use to tell my story that will do a better job than I can?" Perhaps you, too, will create lasting memories for your prospects and clients.

Another idea is to use props as a way of causing the audience to remember you. Some of our clients place their logos on nice pens, notepads, and mint boxes and set these items at each person's place setting before the meeting starts.

Gimmicks

Never use a prop that has nothing to do with your pitch. I attended a program once at which the presenter had a wind-up toy monkey with a cymbal on each hand. Periodically he'd crank up the monkey and it would go clanging away. Although it was funny at first, the periodic clanging of the monkey wasn't relevant to his presentation and served as no more than a distraction.

Backups

Sooner or later you will have an equipment challenge with the current technology. Possibilities include:

- The projector doesn't recognize the computer
- The projector malfunctions

- Your laptop malfunctions
- You drop your laptop
- You lose your laptop

Without a backup, you will not be able to illustrate your presentation with the visual aids that can help you sell your idea, product, or service. Let's take a look at some possible back-up solutions:

- *CD-ROMs, DVDs, and USB flash drives.* Always back up your presentation using one of these tools. If your computer is lost, damaged, or malfunctioning, merely use your backup in another computer.
- *Overhead projector transparencies.* Although overhead projectors are old technology, they are available in many offices. Make a copy of your presentation slides on acetates and take them with you. On the other hand, if you're using this format as your primary method of presentation, you are giving your audience the message that you're not computer-literate. Enhance your perception by upgrading to a laptop computer and projector.
- *35mm slides.* Slide projectors also are old technology but, as with overhead projectors, many offices have one that you can use as a backup. The cost of producing the slides makes this option a more expensive one. However, if you are using 35 mm slides as your presentation method, the same advice applies, upgrade to a laptop computer.

DESIGN GUIDELINES

The Six-by-Six Rule

This rule states that a text slide should have no more than six bullet points and no more than six words in any one bullet point. Many times you'll see slides with line after line of text:

A Violation of the Six-by-Six Rule

You will capture significant cost savings in three primary categories

- **Occupancy Expense Reductions**
    - By restructuring service contracts and dedicated labor, you will achieve **$7.3 million** in occupancy expense reductions over a 36-month period. Primary generation areas include: Continuous application improvements
- **Integrated Labor Model**
    - You will eliminate overlaps and inefficiencies in the use of labor, resulting in **$3.4 million** savings
- **Energy Management**
    - Based on our review of the 2001 energy consumption for a large sampling of your portfolio, you can realize significant savings of **$5.2 million** through better demand management, requiring little to no capital investment.

In this slide, you see a clear violation of the six-by-six rule. Note that each bullet point is an entire sentence. Now let's apply the rule:

Example of the Six-by-Six Rule

Cost Savings

- Occupancy Expenses
- Integrated Labor
- Energy Management

By applying the rule, we've reduced the bullet points to three: occupancy expenses, integrated labor, and energy management. As the presenter, you say all of the information that illustrates each point. Remember, slides are for the audience. They help the audience remember key points. Slides are not for you. Don't use them as your notes or, even worse, as your script. Place your notes on pieces of paper, not on your slides.

Graphics Say It Better

Your audience would prefer to look at graphs, charts, and photos. Taking the same information from the text slides above, we can convert them into more visually appealing charts.

Pie Chart

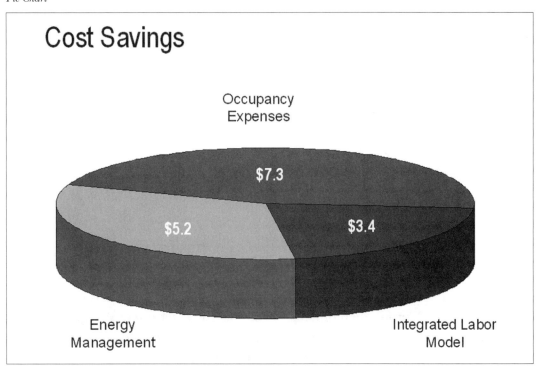

Cost Savings

Occupancy Expenses — $7.3

Integrated Labor Model — $3.4

Energy Management — $5.2

As with text slides, some graphic slides have too much information. In the following example, there are four slides crammed into one slide.

A Slide Containing Four Charts

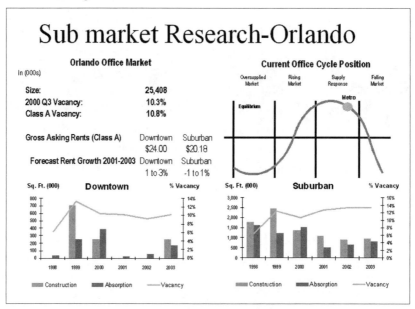

Video Clips Are Powerful

There are numerous uses for video clips, all of which are of excellent edutainment value. If you are giving a team presentation and one of the team members is unable to be at the meeting, record a short videotape of him making some salient points for playback during your pitch.

Another idea is to videotape client testimonials to play at appropriate moments. When the presenter discussed the benefits of working with his firm during a recent pitch, he played a video clip of a satisfied client. His client, the president of a major manufacturing company said, "When we first starting working with ABC Company, our order system was a mess. Within 18 months, not only had they cut our delivery time in half, they reduced our costs by 25 percent. Hiring ABC was the best decision we ever made." Imagine what your closing ratio would be if you had several of these video testimonials throughout your pitch.

Another great idea is to incorporate virtual tours in your pitches. Recently, a commercial real estate firm made a pitch to the managers of a large industrial real estate fund who were interested in disposing of the fund's portfolio of industrial properties. In describing how the commercial real estate team would market the properties, one of the team members took the audience on a helicopter flight beginning at Hartsfield-Jackson Atlanta International Airport, continuing up the interstate, and concluding with a 360° flight around the property. This video clip demonstrated the creative marketing talents of the commercial real estate firm and is one of reasons the firm won the assignment.

All Elements Visible and Accurate

Use 24-point type or larger to ensure that everyone in the room can see your information. For slide presentations, sans serif font is easier to read than serif.

Sans Serif and Serif Fonts

Limit the types of fonts to two, as more will be distracting. Of course, be sure to use the spelling feature on your software program. Importantly, ask someone with a good eye for detail to look for any errors that spell checker might have missed.

No More than Three Colors

When you use too many colors, slides become confusing. Limit slides to no more than three colors. Be sure to recognize the strategic value of colors in your selection.

The Strategic Value of Colors

Color	Impact	How To Use
Black	Neutral, basic	Lettering, borders, outlines
Blue	Promotes creativity, calms mind	Lettering, graphics, soft shapes
Green	Suggests harmony	Lettering, graphics, boxing
Purple	Power, inspiration	Use sparingly, labels
Red	Exciting, stimulates activity	Use sparingly, titles, important info
Brown	Warm, suggests balance	Great for lettering, easily seen
Yellow	Useful for positive thinking	Highlights, auras
Orange	Helps digestion of ideas	Underscore, highlight

Slide with White Bullet Points

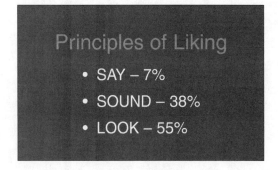

The colors that create the sharpest contrast will be the most important elements. For example, your eyes are drawn to the white bullet points in the following slide.

Introduce Elements at the Appropriate Moment

When you bring up a screen with all of the bullet points you plan to discuss, you will find yourself talking about the first point while the audience is looking at the last. By using the custom animation feature in your presentation software program, you can introduce each element on the screen as you are ready to discuss it. This way you will control what you want the audience to see. As you move from one bullet point to the next, dim the previous bullet point, so that the audience's attention will be drawn to the current point.

Slide with Dimmed Bullet Points

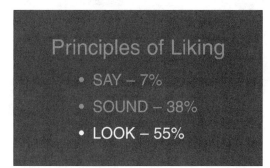

Keep the entry animation consistent. Don't create a distraction by having one bullet point fly in from the right and another zoom from the left. Sounds can be distracting, too. When in doubt, avoid them.

Employ Action Buttons

If you have information to document the points you will make in your pitches, don't put it in your presentations. Remember, don't tell people everything you know. A great way to use supportive information is to place action buttons on the screens that may generate requests for more detail. Then link the action buttons to hidden screens containing supportive information. When you click on the action buttons, you are linked to the screens with the supportive information. When you finish the discussion on those screens, you click action buttons that take you back to the original screens.

Slide with Link Button

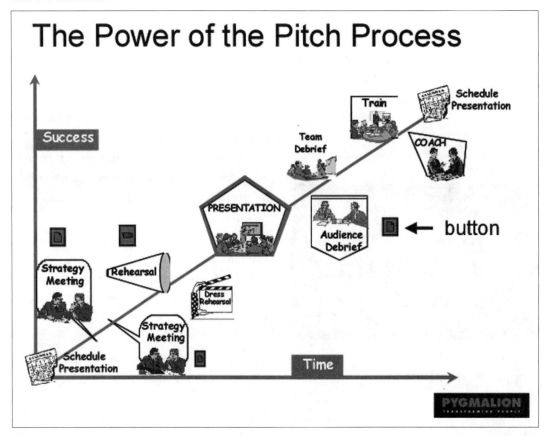

PRESENTATION TIPS

Keep the Lights On

When you use a projector, the natural tendency is to dim or turn off the lights to improve the clarity of the images on the screen. Unfortunately, this also brings the energy level in the room down. Worse yet, people might go to sleep. Keep lights off over the screen and up on you and the audience. In some rooms, you may need to unscrew the light bulb that is located over the screen.

Talk to the Audience, Not to the Visual

Never talk to the screen, flipchart, or any other visual aid you are using. When you do, you exclude the audience from your conversation. Build rapport by always talking to the audience while gesturing to the visual aid. If you're using a laptop computer, glance at the laptop screen for points that you wish to make. This way you can easily maintain an eye connection with your audience.

Point, Then Speak

If you're using a flipchart, point to the information on it, and then speak. Whenever you move and speak at the same time, it takes away from the impact of your words.

Remove Visual after Use

Once you have completed your discussion of a point, which you illustrated with a slide, remove the slide so that the audience doesn't continue to look at it. Click to a black blank slide if you don't have a slide to illustrate your next point. A black blank slide also provides you an excellent means to transition to your next point. The following slide sorter view illustrates the use of transition slides in a presentation.

Use of Transition Slides

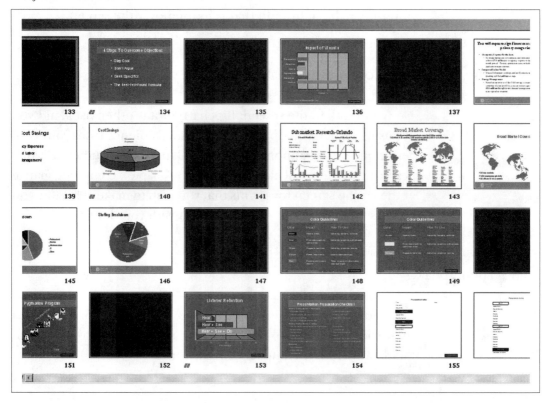

Similarly, remove a board or prop when you no longer need it so that it won't be a distraction when you move to your next point.

Rehearse the Visuals with the Presentation

Be sure that you set up your laptop and projector, and practice using the visuals with your presentation. Perhaps you've seen someone giving a presentation and they'll bring up a screen that they were supposed to have used earlier in the presentation. This is a clear indication that the presenter did not rehearse the presentation with the visuals.

Know the Equipment

Although hardware and software manufacturers have made great progress in simplifying the technology, it can still be tricky. Here are some suggestions to make your life easier.

- Understand how to transfer the image on your laptop screen to the projection screen.
- Know how to use the projector. Take 15 minutes to learn how to adjust the focus, color, and volume.
- Take a presentation software course. Don't be dependant on an assistant or IT professional. What happens when you want to make changes or update information and that person isn't with you? A short three-hour course will give you the competency you need.

Be Prepared to Go on without It

I have come to the conclusion that Murphy's Law was written specifically for presentation software and equipment. What will you do when someone steals your laptop, the backup disc has a virus, and you can't find an overhead projector for the transparencies you brought? Know that at some point this type of disaster will strike, and when it does, let the show go on. Act as if nothing was wrong. Above all, don't apologize to the audience for not having visual aids, they won't even know.

THE MTV SOCIETY

The average television program changes scenes every 20 seconds. For the average MTV program, it's every two seconds. Think about the people sitting in your audience accustomed to a scene change every two to 20 seconds. Now they have to listen to you speak for an hour. How will they act when you are the only scene? They will tune out. They are the MTV Society and they have been conditioned to expect constant visual stimulation. Also, lest this point go unrecognized, you and I are part of this group, too. The MTV Society demands to be entertained. As presenters, we must deliver by incorporating all forms of relevant multimedia in our presentations. Create scene changes with succinct bullet points, photos, graphs, video, animation, flipcharts, and props.

By employing the presentation tips and guidelines in this chapter, you will increase the probabilities of winning more business. Please don't let my words of caution frighten you into avoiding visual aids. My purpose is to help you avoid the countless pitfalls I've encountered over the years. Become an expert in the use of visual aids and watch how your audiences become more engaged. Then watch how your closing ratio skyrockets.

Chapter

15

NOTHING HAPPENS UNTIL YOU CALL SOMEONE

Robert Lewis Stevenson had it right when he said, "Everyone lives by selling something."

The telephone plays a critical role in making pitches in that nothing happens until you call someone. E-mail messages, letters, and faxes won't do it. Chance introductions and meetings might do it. The "it" gets to the purpose of the call: to schedule an appointment.

In this chapter, you'll learn how to make calls that will fill your appointment calendar and provide you the opportunity to make all the pitches you must to meet your goals. We'll devote discussion to the types of calls you make to people you don't know: cold calls. Unlike warm calls, no one has referred you, and except for the possibility of your organization, prospects don't know you exist.

THE PSYCHOLOGY OF COLD CALLS

Most people dread making cold calls, and for good reason. Calling strangers and having conversations with them can be more

203

awkward than meeting people at a networking event. When you meet people face to face, you have the advantage of nonverbal gestures. You feel much more confident about entering into conversations when people look at you and smile as you approach them. In a cold call, you don't have the luxury of facial expression. Your only means of communication is your voice.

You may be asking yourself, "Why would people want to take time out of their busy day to speak with me?" This is a fair question only if you don't have anything of value to offer—in which case, you are wasting their time. It's imperative that you believe that what you are calling about is valuable. If you don't, don't make the call. It may be that you need to find something valuable to call about.

THE PURPOSE OF THE COLD CALL

The purpose of the cold call is to obtain an appointment, period. Don't try to sell anything. Don't have a lengthy conversation about the weather just because someone is willing to talk to you. Schedule a time to meet with the prospect to make your pitch. Then say good-bye, hang up the phone, and call another prospect.

THE ANATOMY OF THE COLD CALL

The I.D.-Benefit Statement

This is where you give a mini version of your elevator speech. This is a statement of who you are and the benefit you provide clients. It might go something like this:

Mrs. Jones, this is Bob Knight of ABC Advisors, we help people protect their estates.

The Reason-Benefit Statement

In this statement you tell prospects how your services or products have benefited other people and that those same products and services could benefit them.

The reason I'm calling is because I recently helped a wealthy family virtually eliminate estate tax. I'm confident that we can do the same for you.

The Request

Now you ask prospects if they would like to meet to discuss how you may be of value to them.

Would you be interested in learning how? Excellent. How about this Thursday at 10:00 AM?

Sometimes it's just that easy, especially if the Reason-Benefit Statement is strong. However, most of the time prospects will have an objection. What they're really saying is that they need to know more before they will invest any more time with you.

HOW TO OVERCOME OBJECTIONS

Frequently, people will have objections after you make the Reason-Benefit Statement. Let's assume you have just said:

The reason I'm calling is because I recently helped a wealthy family virtually eliminate estate tax. I'm confident that we can do the same for you.

The prospect may say something like:

I already have someone taking care of my estate.

Now you can apply the formula for overcoming objections that you learned in Chapter 13: "The Secrets of Building Rapport."

Stay Calm

Remember, prospects want to ensure that you're not going to be wasting their time. Besides, almost anyone you call will have some kind of a relationship with a competitor. Don't be alarmed with this type of statement.

Don't Argue

At all cost, avoid the temptation to debate the statements people make. You never want to hear yourself say something like:

Well, that person may not be as knowledgeable as I am.

This will only lead to an argument:

Prospect: Yes, she is.
You: I don't know her, but I can tell you she isn't.
Prospect: I can tell by speaking with you that she is.

You get the picture. You won't win the argument and the prospect won't see you.

Seek Specifics

This is your opportunity to get more specific about some of the broad objections prospects give you. Ask questions that will give you some idea of whether you can help them or not. You might say something like the following:

So that I can get an idea of how much assistance I might be able to offer, tell me about the services she provides you.

Based on the responses you receive, you may decide you can't help and that you are better off calling more qualified prospects. On the other hand, if you feel you can provide products or services that would be beneficial, use the Feel-Felt-Found Formula.

The Feel-Felt-Found Formula

In our example, let's suppose Mrs. Jones tells you that her sister-in-law is an insurance agent and that she has relied on insurance products to resolve her estate planning needs. In this case, you might respond with:

I understand how you feel, Mrs. Jones. One of my clients, who is also the president of her company, felt equally comfortable with the insurance products she had purchased to meet her estate planning needs. But she found that our Wealth Preservation Program provided a much more comprehensive solution. I would be pleased to spend 30 minutes with you to tell you how it works.

If she agrees, set up the appointment and make your pitch. If she gives you another objection, use the Feel-Felt-Found Formula in a modified form, such as:

I hear what you're saying, one of my clients said she was equally comfortable with the insurance products she had purchased to meet her estate planning needs. But she told me that our Wealth Preservation Program provided a much more comprehensive solution.

RULES OF THE GAME

It's about Your Voice

Because prospects can't see you, your voice initially is the most important factor in making cold calls. As we discussed in Chapter 6: "Put Power in Your Voice," be enthusiastic, but not over-the-top. Use projection, range, inflection, and pace to create interest. Tape record your cold calls and listen carefully to your voice. If prospects don't like your voice, they will attempt to get you off of the phone as soon as possible.

Stand Up

If you sit to make your cold calls, you may slump down in your chair and lose the passion that is so critical to making successful calls. Your voice will have more power if you stand. Gesture just as if you were speaking to the person in the room with you.

Buy a Mirror

I once visited a telephone sales department of a shipping company in Germany and noticed that everyone had a mirror at their desks. When I asked the owner of the company why there were so many mirrors, he told me, "So they can see if they're smiling." He had a significant point. The smile is just as important on the phone as it is in person. Prospects can hear the smile in your voice. Buy a mirror and look at yourself frequently. Smile throughout cold calls and you may hear prospects smiling back at you.

Befriend Gatekeepers

Your prospects' executive assistants can be your best allies. Don't bully, lie to, or mislead them. Explain why you are calling. Your conversation might go like this:

Gatekeeper: Mr. Big's office.

You: This is Bob Knight of ABC Advisors. I would like to speak with Mr. Big.

Gatekeeper: May I tell Mr. Big why you're calling?

You: I help people protect their estates and would like to see if I can help Mr. Big.

This is the kind of conversation you want to have with gatekeepers. Treat them with respect and they can be very helpful. You want them to go to Mr. Big and say, "Oh, Mr. Big, it's that nice Mr. Knight on the phone for you. Would you like to speak with him?"

Don't Play Telephone Tag

Rather than ask prospects to call you back, schedule telephone appointments with them or their assistants. This is an efficient solution to avoiding the dreaded telephone tag. To increase the likelihood that prospects will keep the telephone appointments, use the conference calling service of your telephone company and give prospects toll-free call-in numbers.

Best Times to Call

The best time to call prospects is when you can reach them directly. The decision makers you want to meet with typically work
long hours. Many are workaholics. Typically, the best time to reach
them is early in the morning before the gatekeepers arrive or at
the end of the day after the gatekeepers have gone home.

Leave Voicemail Messages

When prospects aren't in, don't miss the opportunity to let
them know you are attempting to reach them. Leave your I.D.-
Benefit Statement as a voice mail message:

> Mrs. Jones, this is Bob Knight of ABC Advisors, we help
> people protect their estates. Recently, I helped a wealthy fam-
> ily virtually eliminate any estate tax. I'm confident that we can
> do the same for you. The reason I'm calling is to see if you'd
> like to know how. I'll call you back this afternoon at 3:00.

Do not ask prospects to return your call unless you have a relationship with them. It's unlikely prospects will call you back, and
they will consider your request an annoyance. Moreover, you run
the risk of not remembering who the prospect is if you have made
a number of calls that day. I can speak from experience. During
my first year as a stockbroker, I made about 50 cold calls a day.
Whenever a prospect wasn't in, I left a message asking him to return my call.

One afternoon the phone rang, and a man said, "Mr. Hankins,
this is Doug Lamb returning your call." I hesitated for a minute as
I searched my list for Doug Lamb. "Mr. Hankins, are you still
there?"

"Yes, sir," I replied as I attempted to find out who Doug Lamb was and why I had called him. "Just a minute please."

"Mr. Hankins," he said disgustedly, "if this call is so cold that you don't know who I am, our conversation is over." Soon after Mr. Lamb hung up the phone, I located his name and saw my notes indicating that he was one of the most important attorneys in the city.

The Power of Persistence

A year earlier, when I was a trainee going through the securities training program in New York with what was at that time Reynolds Securities, one of our coaches showed me the following statistics on persistence:

- 48 percent quit after the first call.
- 20 percent quit after the second call.
- 7 percent quit after the third call.
- 5 percent quit after the fourth call.
- 20 percent make five or more calls and make 80 percent of the pitches. Only 20 percent of the people who make pitches will call someone five or more times. That 20 percent will meet with 80 percent of their respective target markets. Once again, this is the 80-20 rule at work. Don't give up just because people don't return your calls. They are busy dealing with their own clients and, for the moment, you are not important.

There's another factor that comes into play. Many of the executives you call are or were sales professionals. They may test you to see how good you are. One of my clients, Bill MacDonald, president of Retirement Capital Group, a successful executive benefits consulting company based in San Diego, California, brought this to my attention many years ago when I was meeting with him in his office. During our conversation, his secretary stuck her head in the door and said, "Les Ash is on the phone."

"Tell him I'll call him back," Bill instructed. "I hope he calls back," Bill confided in me. "He has a service we can use."

Somewhat mystified, I asked Bill, "If you can use his service, why don't you return his call?"

Bill's response helped me understand the mentality of the top producer he had become, "I want to see how good a salesman he is."

As a salesman himself, Bill had to prove himself everyday. He expected the same from people who called him.

Don't Be a Broken Record

When you don't reach prospects, change the voicemail messages you leave on the second, third, fourth, and fifth calls. By varying your I.D.-Benefit and Reason-Benefit Statements each time you call, you won't sound like a broken record. Here's an example:

First call: Mrs. Jones, this is Bob Knight of ABC Advisors, we help people protect their estates. Recently, I helped a wealthy family virtually eliminate estate tax. I'm confident that we can do the same for you. The reason I'm calling is to see if you'd like to know how. I'll call you back this afternoon at 3:00.

Second call: Mrs. Jones, this is Bob Knight of ABC Advisors, in our effort to help people protect their estates, I thought you might enjoy reading our recent white paper that discusses some of the pitfalls of estate planning. I'll send it out to you today and check back with you next Tuesday morning.

Third call: I hope you enjoyed our white paper, Mrs. Jones. This is Bob Knight of ABC Advisors. If you haven't already, please take a minute to the read the column on page two that points out the importance of having a wealth advisor who is not paid a commission on products you purchase. I'll check in with you next week to see if we can schedule a convenient time for a brief meeting.

Fourth call: Good morning, Mrs. Jones. This is Bob Knight of ABC Advisors. Our senior economist from New York will be speaking at the Grand Hotel next Thursday evening at 6:00 P.M. His accurate forecasting has been extremely beneficial for our clients. If you'd like to attend, please call me at 1 (800) 546-9000. I look forward to meeting you.

Fifth call: Good afternoon, Mrs. Jones. Sorry you weren't able to attend our economic forecast meeting last evening at the Grand Hotel. I'm sending you a CD-ROM recording of our economist's presentation. I'm sure you'll find it beneficial. Incidentally, I'm still interested in spending a few minutes with you to see how we might be helpful. If you have a minute, please call me at 1 (800) 546-9000 to schedule a convenient time. If I don't hear from you, I'll call you in a few days.

By this time, you've established a relationship with the prospect, even though you've never spoken to her. Your probability of meeting with her is now 80 percent.

Drip on Them Slowly

Don't rush the appointment-making process. You don't want to come across as desperate or needy. When prospects meet your target demographics, call them no more than once a week.

Rejoice with Rejection

At some point prospects will either agree to meet with you or tell you they're not interested, regardless of your ability to overcome their objections. When this happens, thank them politely and hang up the phone. Then say to yourself, "Next!"

THE POWER COLD CALL TOOLKIT

Contact Database Manager

To ensure that you contact prospects when you say you're going to, use a contact database manager such as Goldmine or ACT.

Qualified List of Prospects

Before you start calling, be sure you have a qualified list of prospects that meet your demographic, geographic, and psychographic requirements. As General Norman Schwartzkopf says, you want a "target-rich environment." This preparation step will keep you from wasting a lot of time.

Headset

Save your neck and shoulder by investing in a headset.

Mirror

You'll want to be sure you're smiling.

Marketing Materials

Sending marketing materials to prospects is an excellent way to maintain visibility. Have a good supply of the following:

- Newspaper articles
- Magazine articles
- Testimonial letters
- Market reports
- White papers

Personalized Notes

Have your printer create some note cards that you can attach to the marketing materials you send to prospects. Then handwrite personal messages to accompany these materials. Although this step takes more time than an e-mail message, your correspondence will stand out from the dozens of e-mails prospects receive during the day. And you won't run the risk of having your message deleted.

STAY WITH IT

By following these suggestions, you will schedule more appointments, make more pitches, and close more business. Stay positive. Cold calling is a mental game. Believe that you are offering a valuable product or service and the people you call will believe you and want to meet you. Then you will be able to unleash the power of your pitch.

16

VIRTUAL PITCHES
The Power of Technology

Corporate America is turning more and more to virtual meetings as a way of reducing costs, saving time, and ensuring the safety of their employees. As the newest entrant, Web conferencing has the potential of dwarfing in-person meetings. *Forbes* magazine named WebEx, the largest provider of Web communications services, the Number One Fastest Growing Company in 2003. Gartner Research opined that Microsoft's recent acquisition of Web-conferencing provider Placeware will dramatically change the industry.

In February 2004, InterCall Inc., a division of West Corporation, and one of the largest service providers specializing in conferencing communications, announced a strategic alliance with Microsoft to deliver integrated audio and Web-conferencing services. Conference Place, a co-branded service powered by Microsoft Office Live Meeting, offers flexible Web-conferencing and virtual collaboration solutions. When combined with InterCall's audio conferencing services, Conference Place transforms a phone and a PC with an Internet connection into a virtual conference room.

Frost and Little estimates that Web conferencing will grow from $266 million in 2001 to $2 billion by 2010. Coupled with the ease of use, technological alternatives to live meetings are paving the way for an explosion in the frequency of sales presentations.

The tremendous growth in Web conferencing means that if you're not using this technology to conduct some of your pitches today, you will be soon. The learning curve for using this medium can be steep, so I encourage you to get started today.

In this chapter, we'll discuss how to make a powerful pitch using the three most popular types of virtual meetings: audio conferencing, video conferencing, and Web conferencing.

AUDIO CONFERENCING

Currently, audio conferencing comes in two forms: telephone and Internet telephony. Let's take a look at each one.

Telephone Audio Conferencing

This technology has been around the longest and is the most reliable. There are hundreds of CSPs (conference service providers), from the largest, AT&T, to smaller providers, such as ACT Teleconferencing. Start by inquiring about the services provided by your long-distance carrier. Look for the following features:

- Toll-free dial-in. Remember you will be using teleconferencing to make pitches to clients and prospects. You don't want them to have to pay for the calls.

- Reservation-less system. This way you can schedule conference calls on demand by using a preassigned dial-in number and access code.
- Digital recording. You may want to forward the call to people who weren't able to attend.

Internet Telephony Conferencing

The Internet has created a significant technological breakthrough in teleconferencing in the name of VoIP (Voice-Over-Internet Protocol). VoIP allows you to use the same bandwidth for data and voice communications simultaneously. The big benefit to using this technology is that you can set up a conference call anywhere in the world for free or near free.

You place a voice call either from your computer to a telephone or to another person's computer. When you call computer to computer, you and the other party must have compatible telephony software and be online at the same time. Since there are no universal standards, you and the person you call must use the same software, which you can download free from the Internet. Calling from computer to telephone is simpler, because only you need the software. You'll need a sound card, microphone, and speakers, which most PCs and laptops have pre-installed. If you're in an open office space, you'll also need a headset for privacy.

Because the technology is still relatively new, there are some challenges with the quality of the voice transmission. One is the lag time between when you speak and when the other party hears your voice, known as "latency." The other is voice distortion. Given the importance of your pitch, I recommend that you experiment with Internet Telephony Conferencing, but use Telephone Audio Conferencing for the time being.

TIPS FOR MAKING SUCCESSFUL AUDIO CONFERENCE PITCHES

- E-mail instructions to customers and prospects and confirm that they have the correct dates, times, and call-in numbers.
- E-mail any material that you want people to look at in advance and confirm that they have received it.
- Before you start the call, be sure your office is quiet, that you have silenced any other phone lines, and that you have turned off your cell phone and PDA.
- Start on time. Your prospects and clients are busy, and they don't have the time to discuss the weather or last night's ballgame.
- If you're making the pitch to prospects whom you've never met, ask them to introduce themselves.
- Similarly, ask prospects to state their names whenever they have a question or comment.
- Speak clearly and loudly. Since people can't see you, they will base their perception of you entirely on how you sound and what you say.
- Keep your vocal energy up. Sit up in your chair or stand. Imagine that the people with whom you're speaking are in the same room with you.
- Smile and gesture just as you would do if you were live. Remember the Rock Star Attitude. Give them some love.
- Avoid attempts to be funny. It may not come across well and you run the risk of being misunderstood.
- Don't speak when someone else is speaking. Be polite; wait until the speaker has completed a question or thought.
- Avoid sidebar conversations with teammates at your location. If you discuss a point with one of your teammates, be sure to bring your prospect or client into the conversation.

- End the meeting on time. If you said you would complete your pitch by 10:00 A.M., remind your prospect or client when it's 9:45 A.M. that you only have 15 more minutes.
- After you've completed the call, immediately confirm action items in writing.

VIDEO CONFERENCING

Video-conferencing technology allows two or more people at different locations to see and hear each other at the same time. Since many medium-to-large corporations have room-system video-conferencing capabilities, you may be using this technology now. IP (Internet Protocol) or ISDN (dedicated telephone lines) connections coupled with studio-quality equipment produce excellent full-motion video at 30 frames per second, the same as broadcast television. You can also share documents, including your PowerPoint presentation.

The key issue with room systems is cost. Even though prices are just 25 to 30 percent of what they were three or four years ago, room systems are still expensive. Polycom Inc., the largest manufacturer of video-conferencing equipment with a 52-percent market share, charges $7,500 for a room system per location, excluding the monitor. If you share documents, you'll need an additional monitor. For you to schedule virtual pitches with your clients and prospects, they must also have room systems or be willing to go to one of your locations where you have a system installed.

Rather than purchase, install, and maintain the equipment yourself, consider using the services of conference providers who offer video-conferencing rooms you can rent when you need them. If you are in Chicago and your prospect or client is in Dallas, you would each rent a video-conferencing room in your city. HQ Global Workplaces, for example, offers over 3,000 video-conferencing facilities around the world. The cost for a one-hour meeting for both locations will run you about $450.

TIPS FOR MAKING SUCCESSFUL VIDEO CONFERENCE PITCHES

Most of the same tips relating to in-person pitches apply. Just imagine that your clients or prospects are in the same room with you. The following are some additional pointers:

- To make eye contact with the audience, focus your eyes on the camera. Imagine that the camera lens is a person's eye. As in any pitch, don't let your eyes dart around the room.
- Pay attention to your wardrobe. Avoid white, plaid, stripes, and bold prints, as they will be distracting or too bright.
- Sit or stand still. Too much movement is distracting on a small screen.
- Keep your gestures smaller than normal. The audience won't be able to see your big, broad gestures.

WEB CONFERENCING

Advances in telecommunications technologies and lower costs have created tremendous interest in compressed video systems that transmit information via the Internet using IP and digital telephone networks such as ISDN. You and your clients and prospects will each need a desk or laptop computer, monitor, camera, microphone, and speaker, as well as a software program for transmitting information between your computers. You will be able to see and hear the other person in real time as well as your Power-Point presentation. Documents and PowerPoint slides take up most of the screen, with a smaller window for video. The video component is important because it gives your prospects and clients the ability to see you, which is the most important element of The Principle of Liking.

Screen with Video and PowerPoint

If you find you don't have sufficient bandwidth to support both document sharing and video, you can opt for document sharing only.

Screen with PowerPoint Only

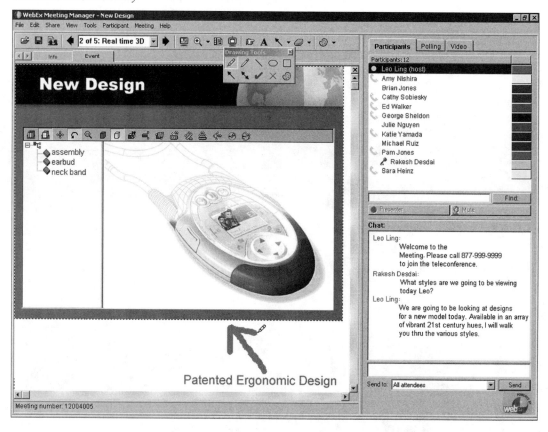

With the support of vendor software technicians, installing and running the programs is relatively painless. The chief obstacle is bandwidth, which describes the capacity of a network or portion of a network. Since the pieces of information that traverse a network are called bits, bandwidth is measured in bits per second (bps), kilobits per second (kbps), and megabits per second (mbps). Since you are running video, data (i.e., your PowerPoint presentation), and audio (VoIP) over the same line, you will need sufficient bandwidth. Without it, video runs at about 15–20 frames per second, thus transmitting jerky movements. Fortunately, the new industry standard, h.264, only requires 128 kbps of bandwidth, which means you should have no difficulty running any part of your Web conference, be it video, audio, or document sharing, as long as your system is h.264 compliant.

As with Internet Telephony Conferencing (VoIP), I recommend that you be thoughtful about how you will use Web conferencing. If you are interested only in video, video conferencing using your own room system or that of a conference provider is the best solution. With Web conferencing, you will have no difficulty running presentation software. But, depending on your available bandwidth, adding audio and/or video may attach an element of uncertainty that you don't need when making a pitch. Before you schedule a Web conference pitch, test the service several times to be sure it's working properly. Our first attempts about two years ago were disastrous. I'm not sure the client has forgiven me yet.

WebEx is the largest Web conferencing provider with a 67-percent market share. The company will set up your own Web-conferencing site and provide you with excellent support. The cost runs from $3,000–$15,000 to set up the system and $100–$250 per month per user thereafter. Minimally, you will need a two-user license, which will allow you to connect with one other computer.

ALWAYS OPT FOR IN-PERSON PITCHES

Regardless of the expense and additional time, meeting with prospects and clients face to face is your best choice. As good as audio, video, and Web conferencing is, you will not benefit from the kinesthetic experience of being in the same room with someone. Only in face-to-face meetings will you and your audiences benefit from the nuances of emotion, touch, and expression. Always look to meet with people in person.

17

THE VIEW IS
WORTH THE CLIMB

Speaking once about his love of mountain climbing, former UN Secretary-General Dag Hammarskjöld said, "Never measure the height of a mountain until you have reached the top. Then you will see how low it was."

Congratulations. By having read this book, you've learned the strategies, tools, and tips for creating powerful pitches. By applying this knowledge, you *will* become a persuasive presenter. Before we close, let's look at some recommendations that will take you to the top of the mountain.

LIVE AND BREATHE THE POWER OF THE PITCH

Keep this book in front of you as a valuable resource. Use it as a tool and review it periodically. One of our clients, Thomas Glanzmann, the former president of Baxter BioScience, calls the ideas in this book the *toolbox*. Whenever he gives a presentation to the press, his senior management team, or plant employees, he takes out the toolbox to help him prepare his message. I encourage you to do the same.

SEEK OPPORTUNITIES TO PRESENT

Assert Yourself in Meetings

If you are introverted, speak up at committee, office, company, and community meetings that you might attend. This will get you out of your comfort zone and give you a chance to practice the skills you learned in this book.

Ask the First Question

Whenever you attend a speech, listen carefully to the speaker; when it's time for Q&A, raise your hand and, when called upon, stand up and ask the first question. By asking the first question and not waiting until others have raised their hands, there's a good chance that the speaker will call on you. This may seem like a bold move, but it has several benefits. By listening to every word the speaker says, you'll improve your listening skills, and you may learn more about the subject than you normally might have. More importantly, you'll build your self-confidence by overcoming any sense of embarrassment.

Include Speaking in Your Business Plan

There are many organizations that would like to have you speak to them. These include service clubs, chambers of commerce, associations, and various community groups. When I first moved to Los Angeles as a young stockbroker, I didn't know anyone and I had no clients. To increase my visibility, I sent letters to the service club program chairs in the city announcing an "Emergency Speakers Bureau." I promised to deliver a qualified speaker (i.e., me) to discuss one of six investment topics of their choosing upon no more than a 24-hour notice. Little did I know how frequently regularly scheduled speakers cancel. Soon I was speaking at least once a week and opening more accounts than anyone else in my office. Although my speeches were informational, my objective was to persuade as many people as I could get in front of to become clients.

These types of public pitches are very powerful. If you haven't already done so, schedule at least one every quarter. Select organizations whose members meet the profile of your target client. When you give your speeches, mention one or more articles, white papers, your newsletter, or other information that people in your audience might find valuable. Offer to provide them with the information if they will write their requests on the back of their business cards. Better yet, provide them with request forms that list the products or services you provide with a place for special requests.

By seeking to persuade larger groups of people, you'll enhance your skills while building your business.

Join Toastmasters

This Newport Beach, California–based international organization is dedicated to helping people improve their communication skills. There are clubs in virtually every city that meet weekly for breakfast, lunch, or dinner. Depending on the size of the club, you will have a chance to give a presentation every two or three months. The part I find extremely valuable is table topics. Every week a Table Topics Master will ask each member to speak impromptu on a topic with no advance warning. She might ask, "Yesterday the president of Pakistan spoke to the UN. What was the theme of his speech?" and then call on you. Even if you didn't hear the speech, you must speak for 90 seconds on the topic. This is a great way to learn how to think on your feet. See the Resources for Toastmasters contact information.

THE 30-DAY COMPETENCY ACHIEVER

Make it your goal not to have to think about articulation, voice inflection, enthusiasm, gestures, or eye contact. Develop your competencies to the point that they come so naturally for you that your focus is not inward, but on connecting with your audience. You will never achieve your full potential as a persuasive presenter until 100 percent of your focus is on your prospect, client, or employees. Let's examine the four steps for achieving competency that comprise the 30-Day Competency Achiever.

30-Day Competency Achiever

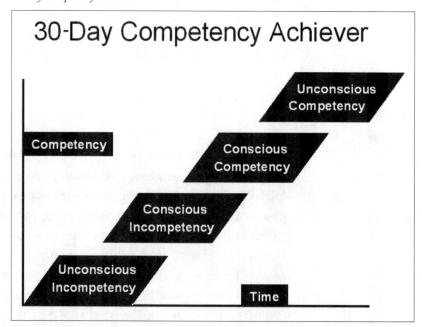

Unconscious Incompetency

On the left-hand axis is competency, and on the bottom axis, time. Before you develop a competency, you have *unconscious incompetency*. It's not that you're a bad person, you just don't have a particular competency, and you don't know that you don't have it. We all start out there, whatever the skill is that we're learning. When we coach clients after videotaping one of their presentations, they're frequently surprised to see that they're not smiling, holding eye contact, gesturing meaningfully, or using any of the many competencies required for making a successful pitch.

Conscious Incompetency

Once you gain awareness, you rise to the level of *conscious incompetency*. This is a much better place to be because now you can do something about it. There are many people in the world who never achieve this second level of competency. Frequently, they're the ones who think they know it all. The great UCLA basketball coach John Wooden was so right when he said, "It's what you learn after you know it all that counts."

Conscious Competency

When you rise to the level of *conscious competency*, you have achieved the competency, but you must think about it all the time. When we point out an area for improvement such as eye contact for a client, he or she can maintain eye contact for two to four seconds, but it requires that person to concentrate on that one skill.

Unconscious Competency

Where you want to be is at the level of *unconscious competency.* This is where you have the competency and don't have to think about it. It just happens for you naturally.

Behavioralists tell us it takes about 30 days of continuous daily practice of a behavior to go from unconscious incompetency to unconscious competency. If you skip a day, you have to start over again. Several years ago, I started taking a multivitamin. Never having taken vitamins much in my life, I found it difficult to remember to take one of the darn pills every day. I took one faithfully the first day, forgot the next two days, remembered the next day and so on for weeks. Before long, I was taking a vitamin daily, and after about 30 days in a row it became a habit. Now I don't even think about it. One of the first things I do in the morning is take a vitamin. It's become an *unconscious competency.*

As you can see, it's vital that you learn about your *unconscious incompetencies.* One of the best ways is to attend a presentation-skills workshop where an instructor will videotape you and point out areas for improvement. An alternative is to videotape yourself giving a presentation and evaluate your presentation. Make a list of the areas for improvement and work on one item each month for 30 consecutive days. By working on one competency every month for 12 months, you will have developed 12 new competencies by the end of the year. That's a tremendous achievement.

As a result of the coaching we gave him in our workshop, one of our clients, Doug McGregor, decided that he was going to work on smiling as the first competency during the 12 months we would be working with him. He confided to me that his six-year-old daughter asked him one day, "Daddy, are you sad?" "No, honey," he responded, "why do you ask?" "You always look sad, Daddy," she replied. Doug said to me, "Whew! Talk about an awakening. I'm so happy we're going to work on this." To ensure that he practiced smiling every day, Doug posted smile stickers on the steering wheel of his car, computer, and cell phone as constant reminders. He instructed his wife, daughter, and secretary to tell him if he was not smiling enough.

I checked in with Doug 30 days later, "How's it going, Doug?" He said, "It's phenomenal! My team tells me how much more open and approachable I am. I feel like I'm connecting more with clients. But the best part is that my family thinks it's great. Maybe it's my imagination, but I feel like I have created a new kind of dynamic in my home. We seem to be so much more happy."

Doug took the advice we gave him to create steps to ensure that he achieved the competency he was working on. You can do this, too.

- Ask for help from your associates, friends, and family.
- Place reminders in visible locations.
- Practice the skill with *every* person you see during the day: your significant other, children, secretary, boss, teammates, vendors, and clients. Don't forget the Starbucks cashier, waitress, dry cleaner, and gas station attendant. This is about every human interaction.

BECOME A STUDENT

Observe professional speakers, politicians, civic leaders, and other professionals when they speak on radio, television, and live venues. If you are near a larger city, attend one of the all-day conferences that feature top speakers from around the world. Pay close attention to how they deliver their messages—eye contact, facial expression, gestures, movement, and vocal quality.

In the Resources section, you'll see a recommended reading list. I encourage you to read all of these books as a way of broadening your knowledge. Check out the resources available at the recommended Web sites. To stay up to date with new strategies and concepts, be sure to sign up for a complimentary subscription to our electronic newsletter.

IT'S UP TO YOU

For you to become a persuasive presenter—to be able to convince people to do what you want them to do—takes knowledge and practice. By having read this book, you have the tools to succeed. Now it's up to you to apply what you have learned. Please take a few minutes to create an action plan by completing the exercise below. Then be sure to follow the plan.

THE POWER OF THE PITCH ACTION PLAN

I will take the following action steps to help me create powerful pitches:

DON'T GIVE UP

Implementing the actions you wrote on your Action Plan will require you to change in many ways. Whenever you change, you experience a variety of emotions.

The Emotional Cycle of Change

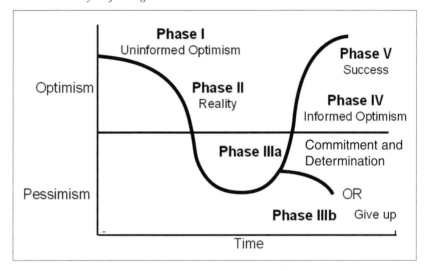

As you contemplate change, you are in Phase I: Uninformed Optimism. You might say to yourself, "The ideas in this book sound great. I'll become a persuasive presenter. I'll close more business. This is going to be great!"

When you begin to implement the items on your Action Plan, you cross the border from optimism to pessimism. Welcome to Phase II: Reality. "I have to make all these changes. I've never done it that way before. This could take a long time."

You become more and more pessimistic as you continue to implement the difficult steps on your Action Plan. Finally, you arrive at a point where you will make a decision. If you take the right fork, you move into Phase III B: Give Up. You will say to yourself,

"This is too much" or "I can't do this" or "I don't have enough time" or "I'm too busy."

If you take the left fork you are in Phase III A: Commitment and Determination. "I can do this. Yes, it's going to take some work. I'll have to make many changes, but I will stick with it."

A few years ago when my daughter Gabi was 10, I took her down her first black diamond ski slope. Although she was a mid-level skier, her confidence had been buoyed by a ski lesson the day before. She said she was ready but asked that I go first. I stopped when I got about halfway down, turned, and looked up the mountain to see how she was doing. It was then that I realized I might have chosen too steep of a run for her. As I watched her carefully maneuver around the moguls, I noticed that she was saying something to herself at every turn. Feeling guilty that I had subjected my daughter to such a difficult task, I was relieved to see that she wasn't crying. Instead of being fearful, she seemed confident as she continued her personal conversation.

When she skied up next to me, I said, "Great job, Gabi. Hey, what were you saying to yourself?"

"I was saying," replied Gabi, "I know I can do it. I know I can do it."

I encourage you to have the same level of commitment and determination that Gabi had that day on the mountain. When you do, you will move into Phase IV: Informed Optimism. As you continue to implement your Action Plan you will reach Phase V: Success.

It will take some time for you to go from Phase I to Phase V. How much time you ask? Give yourself at least a year. But, don't stop then, even if you feel you've mastered the Power of the Pitch. Learning is a lifelong endeavor. If you're like me, you'll find that the more you know, the more you'll want to know.

Implementing your Action Plan won't be easy. Expect some bumps and bruises along the way. I know. Over the past 30 years I've made just about every mistake possible. But, that's part of the journey. As Confucius said, "Our greatest glory is not in never falling, but in rising every time we fall."

It's been a thrill to write this book for you. Now I encourage you to personalize the concepts about how you look, how you sound, and what you say. Make the "toolbox" fit your persona and business. When you do, you will become a persuasive presenter capable of winning more business. Please do me a big favor. As you achieve success with your pitches, take a minute to let me know how you're doing. Please email me at gary.hankins@pygmalioninc.com.

The view *is* worth the climb. I look forward to seeing you at the top.

Ailes, Roger, *You Are The Message.* Homewood: Dow Jones-Irwin, 1988.

Barlow, Janelle, Peta Peter, and Lewis Barlow, *Smart Videoconferencing.* San Francisco: Berrett-Koehler Publishers, Inc., 2002.

Bixler, Suzanne and Nancy Nix-Rice, *The New Professional Image.* Avon: Adams Media Corporation, 1997.

Bohle, Bruce, *American Quotations.* New York: Dodd, Mead & Company, Inc., 1986.

Cohen, Herb, *You Can Negotiate Anything.* New York: Bantam Books, Inc., 1982.

Cooper, Morton, *Change Your Voice, Change Your Life.* New York: Macmillan Publishing Company, 1984.

Ehrlich, Eugene & Hawes, *Speak for Success.* New York: Bantam Books, Inc., 1984.

Elgin, Suzette Haden, *The Gentle Art of Verbal Self Defense.* Englewood Cliffs: Prentice-Hall, Inc., 1980.

Fisher, Roger, and William Ury, *Getting to Yes.* New York: Penguin Group, 1981.

Flusser, Alan, *Clothes and the Man.* 1 ed. New York: Villard Books, 1985.

Gawain, Shakti, *Creative Visualization.* New York: Bantam Books, Inc., 1983.

Gray, John, *Men Are from Mars, Women Are from Venus.* New York: PerfectBound, 2003.

Hagan, Uta, *Respect for Acting*. New York: Macmillan Publishing Company, 1973.

Jackman, Michael, *Business and Economic Quotations*. New York: Macmillan Publishing Company, 1984.

Kushner, Malcolm, *The Light Touch*. 1 ed. New York: Fireside, 1990.

Malloy, John T., *John T. Malloy's New Dress for Success*. New York: Warner Books, Inc./Peter H. Wyden, 1975.

————, *New Women's Dress For Success*. New York: Warner Books, Inc., 1996.

Martin, Phyllis, *Word Watchers Handbook*. 2 ed. New York: St. Martin's Press, Inc., 1982.

Mehrabian, Albert, *Silent Messages*. Belmont: Wadsworth Publishing Company, 1971.

Morrison, Terri, Wyane Conaway, and George A. Borden, Ph.D., *Kiss, Bow, or Shake Hands*. Holbrook: Bob Adams, Inc., 1994.

Murphy, Joseph, *The Power of Your Subconscious Mind*. Englewood Cliffs: Prentice-Hall, Inc., 1963.

Nix-Rice, Nancy, *Looking Good*. 4 ed. Portland: Palmer/Pletsch Publishing, 1996.

Rein, Irving, Philip Dotler, and Martin Stoller, *High Visibility*. New York: Dodd, Mead & Company, Inc., 1987.

Shepherd, Steven, *Videoconferencing Demystified: Making Video Services Work*. New York: McGraw-Hill Companies, 2002.

Simpson, James B., *Simpson's Contemporary Quotations*. Boston: Houghton Mifflin Company, 1988.

Spielman, Sue, and Liz Winfield, *The Conferencing Book*. New York: American Management Association, 2003.

Strunk, William, Jr., and E.B. White, *Elements of Style.* 3 ed. New York: Macmillan Publishing Company, 1979.

Swainson, Bill, *Encarta Book of Quotations.* New York: St. Martin's Press, Inc., 2000.

Tannen, Deborah, *You Just Don't Understand.* New York: Books on Tape, 1993.

Verderber, Rudolf F., *The Challenge of Effective Speaking.* 7 ed. Belmont: Wadsworth Publishing Company, 1988.

Woolf, Bob, *Friendly Persuasion.* 2 ed. New York: The Berkeley Publishing Group, 1990.

AUDIO- AND VIDEO-CONFERENCING EQUIPMENT

Polycom Inc.
http://www.polycom.com

AUDIO-, VIDEO- AND WEB-CONFERENCING SERVICES

ACT Teleconferencing Inc.
http://www.acttel.com

HQ Global Workplaces
http://www.hq.com

InterCall Inc.
http://www.intercall.com

WebEx
http://www.webex.com

HUMOR WEBSITES

http://www.humorx.com
http://www.humorvault.tripod.com/office.html
http://www.ishouldbeworking.com/office.html

http://www.butlerwebs.com/jokes/working.html
http://www.workhumor.com
http://www.halife.com/laughs/office.html
http://www.humorpower.com/articles_free.html
http://www.humorhorizons.com/home.html
http://www.compleatprofessional.com/HumorLinks.html
http://www.humormatters.com'present.html
http://www.mediaprofessional.info/jobhumor.html

QUOTE WEBSITES

http://www.cyber-nation.com/victory/quotations/subjects/
    quotes_subjects_a_to_b.html
http://www.bartleby.com/100/
http://www.quotationspage.com
http://www.quoteland.com
http://www.brainyquote.com

EDUCATION

Toastmasters International
http://www.toastmasters.org

STRATEGIC COACHING

The Strategic Coach Inc.®™ & © 2004
All rights reserved.
Reference in book used with permission.
http://www.strategiccoach.com

WOMEN'S WARDROBES

Mary Lin Dedeaux
Image Consultant
http://www.wardrobeperfect.com

BOOK SUMMARIES

Audio-Tech Business Book Summaries, Inc.
825 75th Street
Suite C
Hinsdale, IL 60521
Phone: 800-776-1910
Fax:: 630-798-7778
http://www.bizbooksummaries.com
(2 summaries a month, $135 a year)

Soundview Executive Book Summaries
10 LaCrue Avenue
Concordville, PA 19331
Phone: 800-521-1227
Fax: 802-453-5062
http://www.summary.com
(3 summaries a month, $89.50 a year)

DOWNLOADS

Please visit our Web site at http://www.pygmalioninc.com to download the following forms:

- The Power of the Pitch 360° Feedback Form
- The Power of the Pitch Questionnaire

- The Power of the Pitch Outline
- The Power of the Outline for Teams
- The Power of the Pitch Audience Debrief Form
- The Power of the Pitch Team Debrief Form

The Power of the Pitch Questionnaire

Presentation Title:

Individual Interviewed: **Title:**

Organization: **Date:**

1. Presentation Team

Name:	Organization:	Title:	Telephone:
Name:	Organization:	Title:	Telephone:
Name:	Organization:	Title:	Telephone:
Name:	Organization:	Title:	Telephone:
Name:	Organization:	Title:	Telephone:
Name:	Organization:	Title:	Telephone:

2. Audience (small group)

Name:	Organization:	Title:	Telephone:
Name:	Organization:	Title:	Telephone:
Name:	Organization:	Title:	Telephone:
Name:	Organization:	Title:	Telephone:
Name:	Organization:	Title:	Telephone:
Name:	Organization:	Title:	Telephone:

The Power of the Pitch Questionnaire, continued

---

3. Audience (large group)

Age:

Male: **Female:**

Annual income:

Education:

Expected attendance:

4. What are the objectives of my/our presentation?

-
-
-
-
-

5. Please identify five challenges faced by your organization.

-
-
-
-
-

6. What are the three most significant events that occurred within your industry/profession or your organization during the past year?

-
-
-

7. Who is your competition?

8. Who are your most important clients?

9. What special jargon or terminology should be used?

10. What issues, events and terms should be avoided?

11. What presentations have you had in the recent past and how were they received?

12. If I were to contact three members of your organization, whom would you suggest? Would you be willing to tell them I might call?

Name:	Organization:	Title:	Telephone:
Name:	Organization:	Title:	Telephone:
Name:	Organization:	Title:	Telephone:

The Power of the Pitch Questionnaire, continued

13. Who are the gurus in your industry/profession?

Name: **Organization:**   **Title:**   **Telephone:**

Name: **Organization:**   **Title:**   **Telephone:**

Name: **Organization:**   **Title:**   **Telephone:**

14. What industry/profession magazines and newsletters do you read?

15. What are the best books about your industry/profession?

16. What questions have we failed to ask that would better help me to understand your organization?

Please send the following information (if available):

☐ **Individual bios (for small audience)**

☐ **Annual report**

☐ **Strategic/marketing plan**

☐ **Mission and vision statements**

☐ **Brochures**

Gary Hankins is the president of Pygma-
lion, Inc., and founder of The Great Communicator Program™,
a comprehensive process that transforms the way CEOs, organizations, entrepreneurs, and sports personalities communicate. A
popular and dynamic speaker, Gary gives speeches to companies
and associations throughout the world. He is consistently rated as
one of the top speakers for such organizations as the Young Presidents Organization, the National Football League, and Club
Managers Association of America.

The genesis of Gary's coaching and speaking career can be
traced to the U.S. Army, where he taught military personnel how
to make winning presentations. He completed his military obliga-
tion as a company commander in Vietnam.

Following his service to his country, Gary became a top producer in the securities industry by speaking to audiences across
the United States and hosting his own radio and television shows.
Then 16 years ago, he realized his passion was speaking, not investing money for people, and that his calling in life was to help
other people become powerful communicators. Today, with more
than 30 years of sales, coaching, and speaking experience, Gary
helps people achieve great success by employing the Pygmalion
Principles of Powerful Communication.

Pygmalion's clients include Jones Lang LaSalle, Deloitte Touche
Tohmatsu, Monrovia Growers, UCLA, Cushman & Wakefield,
The First Bank of Beverly Hill, the San Francisco 49ers, and the
Atlanta Falcons.

When Gary isn't writing, speaking, or coaching clients, he can be found at the beach, boogie boarding with his daughter, Gabi. To contact Gary Hankins:

Pygmalion, Inc.
545 South Figueroa Street
Suite 1227
Los Angeles, CA 90017
213-623-5330
800-PYGMALION
Fax: 213-623-5226
http://www.pygmalioninc.com
gary.hankins@pygmalioninc.com

Share the message!

Bulk discounts
Discounts start at only 10 copies and range from 30% to 55% off retail price based on quantity.

Custom publishing
Private label a cover with your organization's name and logo. Or, tailor information to your needs with a custom pamphlet that highlights specific chapters.

Ancillaries
Workshop outlines, videos, and other products are available on select titles.

Dynamic speakers
Engaging authors are available to share their expertise and insight at your event.

**Call Dearborn Trade Special Sales at
1-800-621-9621, ext. 4444,
or e-mail trade@dearborn.com**